Decoding Early Christianity

Decoding Early Christianity

Truth and Legend in the Early Church

Edited by
Leslie Houlden

with
Graham Gould
Stuart Hall
Stephen Need
and
Lionel Wickham

Greenwood World Publishing
Oxford / Westport, Connecticut
2007

First published by Greenwood World Publishing 2007

1 2 3 4 5 6 7 8 9 10

Introduction and Chapter 1 © Leslie Houlden
Chapter 2 and Chapter 6 © Stephen W. Need
Chapters 3, 7 and 9 © Graham Gould
Chapters 4 and 5 © Stuart G. Hall
Chapter 8 © Lionel Wickham

Leslie Houlden, Stephen W. Need, Graham Gould, Stuart G. Hall and Lionel
Wickham have asserted their right under the Copyright, Designs and Patents
Act 1988 to be identified as the authors of their contributions to this work

Greenwood World Publishing
Wilkinson House
Jordan Hill
Oxford OX2 8EJ
An imprint of Greenwood Publishing Group, Inc
www.greenwood.com

British Library Cataloguing-in-Publication Data: a catalogue record for this
book is available from the British Library

Library of Congress Cataloguing-in-Publication Data: a catalogue record for
this book is available from the Library of Congress

ISBN 978-1-84645-018-1

Designed by Fraser Muggeridge studio
Typeset by TexTech   .
Printed and bound by South China Printing Company

Contents

Introduction

Any book that manages to sell copies on the scale of Dan Brown's *The Da Vinci Code* deserves notice from anyone who has some useful comments to make. This collection of essays aims to make such comments from the side of the study of the documents, events and people who figure in early Christianity. The contributors are all people who are and have been involved in academic life, with sufficient experience to take a wide view of some of the issues that emerge. Not that this book is a collection of vigorous refutations and corrections from people who know better than Dan Brown. That task has been done already, with admirable clarity and economy, by Bart D. Ehrman, in his *Truth and Fiction in the Da Vinci Code* (OUP 2004), which leaves the reader amply aware of the multitude of historical errors and other misconceptions that are to be found in the novel. Ehrman's book is warmly recommended as a critique that the scholarly world in general would endorse; and note, Ehrman is no kind of propagandist on behalf of, for example, churches or other causes that might well think themselves strangely treated by Brown.

Perhaps the first matter on which to be clear is the status of those historical errors or rather the status of the historical statements, whether true or false, made in the course of Brown's book. It is of course a work of fiction, but this has not prevented many readers from taking it as if it were fact or, at least, as if there were 'something in it'. Moreover, Brown does make quite substantial claims for his own accuracy in matters of context and background that do not exactly stand up to scrutiny. We shall comment on the resulting scandalized reactions later. At this point, it is necessary to recognize that the errors, both harmless and scandalous, are mostly placed on the lips of two characters. One, Leigh Teabing, is an eccentric, wildly rich English toff, highly voluble on his obsessive interests, chiefly the location of the Grail and surrounding matters. The other is Robert Langdon, an American academic expert in religious symbology, but with a distinctly shaky penumbra of information about other allegedly related matters. Langdon shows himself only too ready to echo the proposals thrown out by Teabing. The latter turns out to have all the features of a fanatic, ready to take his obsessions to the point of a quadruple murder without hesitation and with a head full of wild conspiratorial notions. There is nothing to suggest that the concoctions of these minds are at all worthy of serious regard. Except for one thing: they may strike many readers with the realization that, while the assertions that emerge from the mouths of these two leading characters look phoney, they themselves cannot be quite sure of what is more likely to be the truth of the matters in question! That is where the present book hopes to assist. Standing back from the novel itself (and certainly from the wild claims that abound in it), it hopes to provide information about some of the main topics in relation to the life of Jesus and the subsequent period of the early Church's life that will be more reliable – or, where necessary, sensibly sceptical. As we shall see, there are many matters in this area of study which must remain uncertain and probably simply unknowable – for lack of evidence in connection with events and people that left little or no public record, even when in subsequent years they have become of the greatest importance to many people. This is notoriously true of the career of Jesus himself. It is not in the least surprising that, where evidence fails, imagination often takes over. And of course some imaginings may be much more sensible than others, with plausible known historical bases. So there is no sense in the response: 'Oh, I see, I recognize that X is foolish, but then, is not all that is said about these matters equally foolish? A plague on all your houses!' Let us be more cautious: a plague on one house is certainly no justification for a plague on all – even though something like contagion in not unknown in such cases!

At this point, it is sensible to tackle another related matter. Much of the hostile response (not unlike that which *Satanic Verses* caused in Muslim circles) to *The Da Vinci Code* has come, not surprisingly, from conservative Christians who have felt affronted by what seemed to them outrageous, even blasphemous, assertions (most of them far from new) about Jesus and the corrupt character of the Bible. The early Church, so the claim goes, actively suppressed the truth about Jesus in the interests of its prejudices and dogmas, chiefly of a strongly patriarchal brand, and accepted only those documents that supported their own case, suppressing or adjusting others. What Jesus actually stood for, in the eyes of those who were his contemporaries, is less than clear – except that he was, we are to believe, glad to be married to Mary Magdalene and to establish a dynasty to perpetuate his (apparently skimpy) theology centred on the feminine principle and a kind of fertility cult, along well-known lines. The reader is then presented with only two options: the benighted content of traditional Christians teaching, starting from the writings found in the New Testament, and the now-unearthed picture of Jesus and what was supposed to come from him but, with transient and only partial exceptions, has scarcely been allowed to see the light of day – and has remained known only to obscure circles of devotees, often persecuted and reduced to the utmost secrecy.

Now it is true that the New Testament is the literature of the winners, and in the first three centuries there was indeed a wide range of beliefs and practices stemming somehow, by all kinds of routes, from Jesus. But there is little doubt that the books of the New Testament are the earliest Christian writings – and themselves represent a wider range of ideas and groups than has often been supposed. It is also true that the sceptical critic may well say: you essay writers are yourselves untrustworthy for you all have an investment of some kind in the traditional picture – that purveyed by history's winners. We must admit that there are indeed Christian scholars who, with the greatest depth of technical scholarship, do give the impression that the argument must come out at 'the right place' – that of traditional orthodoxy, as it has come to be received. But there are many others whose critical stance owes more to neutral methods of argument and evidence-scrutiny than that brand suggests. The history of scholarship in these matters is long and sometimes painful, especially perhaps in Protestant Germany and Catholic France – and, in some cases, in the United States. It is in any case more a matter of history than of present conditions. On the whole, the treatment of British scholars at the hands of church authorities has been gentler – for a variety of reasons; partly because the public concern over such matters has not often been sufficiently strong, and partly because the work has been conducted in the context of the British universities where it has lived alongside other disciplines and been exposed to their scrutiny, however well or ill informed that might be: at least it would be unlikely to stand for illiberal behaviour. There has, in other words, been a respect for standards of evidence which has itself seemed a godly duty, whatever the results might turn out to be. Of course, there has from time to time been a tussle of loyalties, but the common response has been to hold to the leading of the evidence, however unwelcome the conclusions may sometimes be – and this for religious reasons: how can God be honoured by the perversion of the leading of truth? In any case, scholarship in these areas has not been limited to Christian believers.

The essays in this book are not as bound to the details of the novel as Bart Ehrman has been: he went for the informative and detailed rebuttal of the leading inaccuracies and grotesque proposals to be found there. Here we stand back a little and present the reader with what we hope is a dependable guide to the state of affairs in current scholarship with regard to some of the main areas of early Christian life and thought that come up for discussion in relation to the novel. Several of the contributions represent areas in which disputes abound; where this is so they take positions that would be widely accepted as mainstream or, if controversial, at least within the limits of recognized discussion.

We are all of a critical disposition, in the technical sense: we shy away from propaganda and seek to follow the evidence where it seems to lead. We are also ready to change our picture of the Christian past where new paradigms appear to have virtue and the old need to be jettisoned. As will emerge, brand new evidence appears from time to time: in the past century, both the Dead Sea Scrolls and the Nag Hammadi finds, both coming to light in the 1940s, have revolutionized our picture of the Judaism of the time of Jesus in the case of the former, and our knowledge of the ideas of influential Christian minority groups in the early centuries in the case of the latter (see Chapters 6 and 4). Both these discoveries appear in the novel but with highly inaccurate estimates of their character and significance: the former find is said to be of Christian, not Jewish, documents (they are not); and to give information about Jesus (they do not). And the latter set of writings is seen as representing something like mainstream early Christian thought, instead of a group of movements that won the allegiance of a number of thoughtful speculative Christians in the second and third centuries.

But mostly, academic movement in this area is less a matter of brand-new evidence than of new angles of vision from which the material is surveyed. Thus, in recent years, there has been greater candour in viewing the early Church less from the point of view of its later position of strength and more in relation to the social and intellectual situation that it occupied in the period in question. It now seems important to see these men and women and the movements of thought and life to be found among them in the light of their times, including the changing social and political situations in the various parts of the Roman Empire. For a picture of the diversity and the reasons why it came to be severely reduced in the fourth century and after, see now Bart Ehrman, *Lost Christianities* (OUP, 2003). It is apparent that the 'officialization' and disciplining of the central church organization from the time of Constantine (see Chapter 9) brought about a relative standardizing of Christianity and of its picture of itself and of its history which we can now fill out with more justice to its rich variety. But none of this affects our understanding of the actual origins of the movement in the time of Jesus: we can look at that in its own right too and not through the diverse lenses that came into service in the period that followed and, with innumerable variations, have marked much Christian life, for good and ill, down to the present. These essays offer a sort of purge, for the purifying of the system!

Leslie Houlden is a Fellow and Professor Emeritus at King's College London, London, England. He is the author of a number of highly regarded works on the subject of Jesus and the New Testament, including *The Bible and Belief* (SPCK, 1991), *What Did the First Christians Believe?* (Lutterworth, 2000) and *The Strange Story of the Gospels* (SPCK, 2002) and was editor of the encyclopedia *Jesus in History, Thought and Culture* [ABC-CLIO, 2003, now in paperback, *Jesus, the Complete Guide* (Continuum, 2005)]. A former editor of the journal *Theology*, he was made a Lambeth Doctor of Divinity by the Archbishop of Canterbury in 2005.

Stephen Need is Visiting Professor of Theology at St George's College, Jerusalem.

Stuart Hall is Professor of Theology at St Andrew's University, Scotland.

Graham Gould, formerly Lecturer in Church History at King's College, London, is a freelance writer.

Lionel Wickham, formerly of the Faculty of Divinity at Cambridge University, is a freelance writer.

Chapter 1
What Did Jesus Do and Teach?

Leslie Houlden

In a way, it is a hopeless game, this quest for 'the truth' about the life of Jesus. For centuries it was straightforward for the great mass of Christians at least. There it was, in the 'true' accounts in the four gospels. Of course attentive people knew that there were inconsistencies, but there were ways of ironing them out and in any case they did not seem to be extensive. But in the last two or three centuries, the combination of the growth of scepticism, the sense that one had permission to ask searching questions and the unstoppable growth in historical imagination (things were different in those days) has inevitably led to any amount of questioning and theory-making about the subject.

Yet it is an odd situation. There has been little decline, among at any rate believers, in either a general sense that the content of the gospels is (broadly) true – and it would be pretty dreadful for faith if it were not so – or, among some Christians, a fervent conviction that every detail is correct and must be defended to the end. Yet you do get some strange situations.

I recall a day some time in the later 1980s, at a meeting of the Church of England's General Synod, when there was a scene that was at once unedifying and puzzling. There was a debate whose purpose seemed to be to 'deal with' David Jenkins, Bishop of Durham, for his candidly expressed sceptical views about gospel stories, notably, it seemed, about the resurrection of Jesus. There was a nasty baying for his blood from the solid Christian citizens – and it reduced the Bishop to tears. It was something of a disgrace, but felt by the fervent to be no more than was decent. But then there followed a speech by Fr Barnabas Lindars, wearing his habit as a Franciscan friar. Since departed this life, he was Professor of New Testament Studies at the University of Manchester. He got up and told us, quietly and straightforwardly, that there were only a handful of things we could be really and truly sure of about the life of Jesus (I think he mentioned three!). He was heard in silence and with total respect. I came away totally mystified. Was it that bishops must be orthodox but you could give up on professors? Or was it that you could not believe that the words of a holy man in a religious habit could be anything other than a source of truth, to be received with a kind of reverence? Or was it shock? – You just could not believe your ears! I never discovered the answer to my questions, but it was a strange experience. First the atmosphere of the coliseum, baying for blood; then the atmosphere of the lecture theatre, even the church. Somebody should have conducted a survey, there and then. And we might muse that the Franciscan who claimed to be sure of so little, by the fact of his professed lifestyle, derived from the man of Assisi, spoke volumes of the truth about Jesus that shame us all.

There is little doubt that our society, and even the Church, includes every sort of opinion on the matter of the gospels – and not a great deal of knowledge of the issues at stake or the nature of the evidence. Let us begin with a few home truths about the possibilities before us – in the nature of things. First, we are dealing with events of a long time ago, and little checking of evidence is possible and little new evidence is at all likely (despite occasional bits of archaeology that raise a flurry). Second, we are dealing with obscure events: this is not the life of a figure widely prominent in his own day. So he is not someone whom the cool historians of the time would have heard of or dreamt of investigating and assessing, even with the kinds of objectivity that were possible at the time. But third, this is a person who, in the limited circles in which he was known, aroused deep emotions – of both devotion and hostility. There is nothing coolly objective about him or about those reacting to him. Fourth, the only significant evidence we have of him is the work of supporters, the writers of the gospels, and it dates from forty to sixty years after his death. Moreover, these men were pretty clearly not just partial witnesses, with a message to communicate as well as a story, but anxious to present their own (different) views of his nature and purpose. It is moreover maddening that their only predecessor as a Christian writer, Paul the apostle, did not think it desirable or necessary to record anything much about the life of the one who was the centre of his life and work: that in itself can merit a good deal of pondering – at least in a time like our own when people are keen to know 'the facts'. Paul was no co-operator with modern taste! Fifth, there is what might be called the question of prose or poetry. Modern people, whether believers or unbelievers, with their fact-orientated instincts, are uncomfortable to learn that books like the gospels, and the minds that produced them and first heard them, may have had no such hang-ups. Perhaps the gospel-writers moved with ease from what we might call the facts of a case to its meaning, expressing the latter in terms of their imaginative 'take' on the former. And that imagination is of course formed by the writer's own mentality, often created by the images and language – in fact the 'world' – of the Jewish scriptures (hence 'poetry' rather than 'prose', in my shorthand).

An extreme example might be the stories of Jesus' temptations or testings by Satan in the wilderness after his baptism by John, to be found in the first three gospels. The first gospel writer (Mark) gave a brief account of the episode, that is itself full of symbolic elements (Mark 1.12–13): the forty-day period reminds us of Israel's wilderness sojourn under Moses, marked by endless testing, en route to the Promised Land; and then Jesus our Moses, leading us to a greater 'land of promise', takes the mantle of Adam in Eden (which Paul had already conferred upon him), with beasts and angels around him, as at the start of Genesis. In other words, Mark had already told the story (clothed the idea) in poetic images, and we may suppose that he was not in the least worried by the (irritating!) question: Did it happen just so? Matthew and Luke (in each case, the start of Chapter 4) take the matter further (write new poems on the theme?). Jesus was tempted: so what precisely was the content of his temptations? We shall tell you: they were three, and, given Mark's hint, it was natural for them to take up themes from the trials of Israel in the forty-year wilderness wanderings. These writers are poets (with disciplined resources of imagination in their locker). Yet Matthew and Luke give no warning of their taking up that role (in fact they had exercised it lavishly in their first two chapters on Jesus' birth). But why should they? One might say that we ought to know that if you write about God or speak about God, prose is not your medium, 'facts' not your overriding concern: even though you might get squeamish to be examined on where you draw the line between prose and poetry, facts and interpretation. The Franciscan in the General Synod was right: if you want 'facts', then you cannot have many: Jesus came, lived, died – had a ministry of broadly this or that character, proclaimed the 'kingdom of God' and God's imminent fulfilment of that rule of heaven in human affairs. The rest that we read in the gospels doubtless owes much to him, to his teaching and his deeds, but it is not possible to know for sure what or how much – or with precisely what 'flavour' he acted or spoke, years before the stories were written out.

But then, what else would have been possible? What else is possible now? The Battle of Trafalgar was a mere two hundred years ago, and we kept the anniversary in 2005. We were bombarded with books telling its story – all differing about its proper interpretation. All the writers knew 'the facts', but brought to them their own standpoints – we might say also their own poetry. The same is true of any episode in the past or present. We interpret as we speak, indeed as we see or hear: we bring our own 'poetry' to bear on the matter, and the more significant it is for us, the more keenly and inevitably we shall do it. To suppose that the gospel writers gave us 'the plain facts' (whatever that could possibly mean) would be to accuse them of not minding much what Jesus did or taught or stood for: a strange doctrine indeed.

Does this mean that there is a whiff of an accusation of blatant propaganda in the air? Well, propaganda is, we might say, the view we disagree with – but, surely, as presented crudely and with a measure of flagrant dishonesty and of putting one over on the public. There is no need to accuse the evangelists of that, any more than the Trafalgar scholars: though their two kinds of 'poetry' are very different, for they write out of different contexts of imagery and writing.

Much of this might be taken to be an elaborate way of introducing the discomforting message that what we read in the gospels never happened. This would be a wholly faulty conclusion. There can be no sensible doubt that the depiction in the gospels is, with a number of qualifications, a generally credible picture of Palestinian life, politics and culture in the first century of our era. But it remains true that all has been filtered through perhaps numerous minds and imaginations to reach the four books that are before us. And the accounts that we read are works of considerable subtlety – often of kinds that are alien to our customs of thought and writing. Above all, the purpose of our writers was not that a modern passion for high standards of historical accuracy should be satisfied but that the good news concerning Jesus should be made known to their readers – consciously, we must suppose, to those of their own day, but in effect, as things have turned out, to those of all days and all places. It is no wonder that people have always read and imagined as their culture has made it possible for them to do so. The irony is that perhaps literalistic Western men and women are among those least well placed to get anywhere near to the kinds of response that these old documents sought to stimulate.

But then: is it different with Jesus' teaching? It seems not to be so. Matthew, for example, did not hesitate to amend teaching he had found in Mark: see, for example, his provision of an exception clause to Jesus' teaching on divorce (Mark 10.1–10 and Matthew 19.1–10). Are we to believe that he knew for certain that Jesus had not in fact taught what Mark said he had taught? Or, as a church leader, was it that he sought the endorsement of Jesus for the teaching that he himself had come to feel necessary in the circumstances of the church life that he knew? Maybe he thought he was doing no more than add a rider to what he found in Mark, altering nothing in principle: but then to us it seems that he exchanges one vision for another, with Mark showing Jesus presenting a picture of life in the kingdom of God as a mirror for God's purpose shown in Genesis 2 and Matthew making workable rules for 'real life' as it must be lived: showing himself a man of affairs rather than a man of theological vision.

We turn, however, to passages, for example in Matthew 5–7 (the Sermon on the Mount) where Matthew reports teaching that is anything but the product of an administrative mind; on the contrary it is idealistic in the extreme, lifting the heart to God – making us feel 'if only the world, if only we, were like this in our attitudes and behaviour'. (Incidentally, those many people who claim they live by the simple teaching of the Sermon on the Mount are claiming much indeed!)

We could go on for ever discussing both general principles and detailed examples in the gospels. All of them stem somehow from Jesus, but the moves and shifts that have occurred between him and the writings that we have must, in the nature of things, be so many and various that we cannot easily tell how far the natural quest for authenticity can be satisfied. And supposing it could: what would we then do? And where would we draw lines in the matter of legitimate adaptation? In any case, the Christian religion has never acted as if it truly claimed to fix Jesus' message in aspic on all matters. Always it has, by design or by default, acted as if it were all in favour of adaptation and application to new circumstances, wholly different from those of Jesus. What is more, Christian belief has, in its doctrine of the guiding Holy Spirit, always worked with a principle that not only tolerated but positively welcomed movement and adaptation. Of course, this principle has frequently vied with the opposite, brutally conservative tendency; and sometimes revolution has resulted (but more often, admittedly, various kinds of stagnation). But in all circumstances, there has never been a time when the gospels' voices have not been heard and the impact of Jesus' words and deeds has not been felt, often with silent adaptation to new circumstances, even among those most conservative in their conviction. Most obviously, in most of the Christian period, Jesus' teaching on the renunciation of wealth, though constantly repeated, has been largely honoured in the breach, despite the numerous examples of heroic generosity of heart and goods.

It is time to turn from these rather general reflections on the conditions that beset any attempt to achieve a picture of a figure or episode of the past, and especially where Jesus of Nazareth is concerned, and to survey the possibilities that have been canvassed in modern times. In the recent period, Jesus has been the subject of any number of large-scale studies (the year 2000 prompted a particularly strong rich crop).

Many of them start from what may be regarded as more objective matters, such as the context of his life as a person living as a Jew in Palestine in the first century, within the Roman Empire. The recent past has seen a notable growth in knowledge on many relevant matters, notably of the Judaism of Jesus' time.

Most notably, there has been the discovery of the Dead Sea Scrolls, the writings of a hitherto shadowy group of sectarian Jews, some of them their own, others copies of scriptural books. There has been much speculation about possible relations between this group of devout and learned Jews and the movement initiated by Jesus. Not surprisingly, there are similarities between the two groups, but positive overlaps and contacts of a personal or institutional kind are not easy to identify with assurance and it seems most likely that the two groups or movements simply had certain tendencies in common. Both were Jewish reformist groups, both had a strong sense of destiny within a world of apocalyptic speculation, both were involved in the study and interpretation of the old Scriptures, and both were critical of aspects of the existing Jewish establishment. But the movement centred on Qumran and the people of the Scrolls antedated the Jesus-movement by a couple of centuries and it was extinct before the gospels were written. The early Christian writings show no direct knowledge of the Qumran sect, and links with both John the Baptist and Jesus himself are wholly speculative, whatever the similarities between some aspects of their conduct and thought. Most strikingly, we have no evidence of the Jesus-movement including any monastic establishment like Qumran in its early days. Sectarian it no doubt was, but its location was in the towns of Palestine and soon the Roman world at large, and its disposition was missionary not chiefly scholastic, for all the creative interpretation of texts from the Jewish Scriptures that is found in the Church's early writings – notably the Gospels of Matthew and John and some of the letters of Paul (see Chapter 6).

There has also been much work on clarifying the character of more mainstream Judaism in the context of the Palestine of the first century, within the Roman Empire but divided for everyday political and administrative purposes between direct Roman government and the sons of Herod the Great, who ruled the area of Galilee where Jesus was brought up and where he conducted the greater part of his work. So how are we to view that work and how are we to identify him as a historical figure? Well, it is evident that the teaching of Jesus brings before us a world that is wholly in tune with what is known of social relations at the time. The parables, for example, are full of the dominant social pattern, usually described as the patron – client relationship: that is, the relations between creditor and debtor, employer and employed, richer and poorer – which was always likely to be in a state of potential if not actual unease. It is a social setting that was mostly small-scale, personally close and full of opportunity for negotiation and disruption. Most of Jesus' parables exemplify this society with vivid clarity. Others, of course, especially in the Gospel of Mark, are centred on nature and agriculture, notably the parable of the sower, which plays such a pivotal part in the imagery of that Gospel, with its terms echoing elsewhere, if we keep our ears open.

But the fact that Jesus and the gospels so readily 'fit' into the society and world of their time does not of itself tell us very much about Jesus himself. For that we need to have a wider picture of the possibilities available for such a man to be intelligible in that world. What kind of figure could Jesus have been to make sense to the Jews of the Palestine of his day? Especially in the past century and a half, there has been a series of refined suggestions of how Jesus as a historical figure can best be seen in that context. There is wide agreement that the widespread eschatological concern, not to say fever, in the Judaism of the time, with its extravagant apocalyptic speculation, was shared by Jesus. Indeed it is one of the puzzles of early Christianity that it survived the disappointment of those vivid expectations and was able to concern itself efficiently with the ordering of life in the social world of the time. But surely Jesus was not so apocalyptically possessed that he did not also teach about ordinary situations in the present age, as the gospels (especially Matthew and Luke) portray him as doing. We can see not only from the Qumran community but also, in the Christian case, from the letters of Paul that it was perfectly possible for an apocalyptic mindset with all its fervid hopes and expectations for an imminent future to be combined with provision for the needs of ordinary life, whatever qualifications the latter might impose. In other words, an apocalyptic outlook did not produce sheer anarchy. For example, in 1 Corinthians 7, Paul's detailed instructions for a range of marital situations are consciously affected by the short-term provision that seemed to him to be needed; but this does not in the least deter him from taking great care and showing great subtlety in his counsel and his rulings for life as it is.

For another example of the same point: Jesus' overriding theme, announced forcibly in Mark 1.14f., is the nearness of the 'kingdom of God', that is to say his active and visible rule – it was a prime image of apocalyptic hope. Many of the parables of Jesus speak of its imminence, and there can be little doubt that it was the motive force in many of Jesus' reported acts: healings, feedings, liberations, recoveries of various kinds. And in a few statements, we meet the claim that in Jesus' ministry, the kingdom of God is already present: Matthew 12.28; Luke. 11.20. It is hard not to believe that this note was certainly present in Jesus' work and that it was one of the chief factors and idioms of expression that gave him his prominence and his force. Yet we find that it did not deter him from being represented as providing guidance for everyday problems – whose relevance might be seen as of limited duration. Much ink has been spilt on the apparent inconsistencies here, but that worry fails to grasp the poetic character of the spirit that was engendered. We may note that all through Christian history, revivals of apocalyptic hope have come and gone, but the faith they witnessed to and which was, on paper, disappointed did not disappear – it adapted itself to calmer circumstances. Such adaptation can in fact be seen pretty clearly already in some of the later books of the New Testament, such as 1 & 2 Timothy and Titus, written by somewhat later followers of Paul.

For all the agreement on this basic feature of the current consciousness in Jesus' day and in his social setting, there are still numerous different analyses of the precise character of his teaching and ministry. Does one put the emphasis on his healings, for example, or on his everyday teaching? What does one decide to think about the alleged miracles? How far was he what we might see as political in his interests and motivation? This last question is one of the easiest to answer. He seems to have had little desire to overthrow authorities or even to criticize their conduct, as John the Baptist had done – bringing about his own death (Mark 6.14–29). His one reported saying on the subject is cautious (Mark 12.13–17): 'Render to Caesar that which is Caesar's and to God that which is God's'. Unless it was rather evidence of principled astuteness: 'You should know that all things are God's' – in other words, it was Jesus speaking wholly in line with his central preaching of the kingdom of God, at least for those who had ears to hear.

But Jesus may well have been 'political' in a rather different sense. That is, perhaps he really was concerned less with the prospect of the future of mankind in general than with the future of Israel: in other words, like other Jews who emerged in the period, even if he was less violent in his tactics, he was concerned with the renewal of the nation under God's sovereignty. On such a view, the target would be not so much, in the first place, the political leaders (whether Roman or Herodian) as the religious establishment. A puzzle with this view is that it is only in his final days that the gospels show him as showing much interest in such matters. In the main period of his ministry, his controversies are either with those guilty of social evils or with Pharisees and scribes, in other words about issues of interpretation of the Law of Judaism and of scriptural interpretation. Only at the end, do we have a concern with the religious establishment, centred on the Temple at Jerusalem, with its priestly authorities. It is certainly common to see the action commonly called the Cleansing of the Temple (Mark 11.15–19) as both the sealing of Jesus' fate and the revealing of his central policy. In the words that begin the apocalyptic discourse in Mark 13, we see an even more radical statement of what Jesus' policy might have been (vv.1–2). But it is remarkable in that case how little evidence of such a view makes any appearance in the earlier part of the story, apart from the setting aside of twelve men as a central group of followers – which certainly seems to point of a 'restoration of Israel policy'. And it has been sensibly asked how much of a stir would in fact have been caused, in the vast expanse of the outer Court of the Temple, filled by pilgrims at Passover time, by a minor scuffle, such as Jesus seems to have been involved in. It might have seemed to followers of Jesus crucial in retrospect, and as the proximate cause of his arrest, but it is not easy to see how it can have made much impact at the time, even in the context of a touchy regime determined to suppress signs of disorder and seditious teaching.

By contrast, there has been the development of a view of Jesus which centres on the future of Israel, its reform and restoration by God, in line with prophetic tradition and apocalyptic hopes, as subsequent church acclimatizing of Jesus to central Jewish concerns, especially in the decades after Jesus' lifetime. No, Jesus was a teacher of human equality and simplicity of life, centred on fellowship meals, where people of all classes should come together in peace. Especially was he the friend of the outcast and the poor, a former of circles of love and acceptance. He sought to realize the kingdom of God in the midst of a reformed society where people would recognize their common creaturehood under God. His affiliations should be sought among Cynic philosophers of his day, to whom he was strikingly similar, even if it is not easy to demonstrate how a poor Galilean peasant is likely to have come under their direct influence. It is a view that has a certain obvious attraction for liberal-minded modern people, avoiding the inconvenience of 'miracles' and supernatural theories about the imminent future.

Alongside the range of emphases seen in Jesus as presented in the gospels and when seen against his setting in first-century Palestinian Judaism, there is another whole approach to the question of 'identifying' him which focuses more directly on the gospels as documents of their time. What tools can we bring to bear on their analysis and interpretation? Not surprisingly, this subject has its own history, but we may see its various phases as a set of interrogations.

So: one can ask of these short books: What is the relation between you? Clearly you are not wholly independent of each other, but how are we to view your similarities and differences, including your flat contradictions? Over the last two centuries when this has been a lively issue, and the ideas of mere complementarity or ultimate harmony have seemed inadequate, there has been a certain growing together, something approaching general agreement. First, and most widely agreed of all, the belief that the first three gospels do indeed share a great deal of material or at any rate items of material, and that this has to be explained in terms of the order and character of their composition. At this point, of all possible theories, it seems much the most probable of the various possibilities that Mark, the briefest gospel, was written first and that the writers of Matthew and Luke used Mark as their primary source. It is interesting, incidentally, that it has virtually come to be taken for granted that none of the gospels is contemporary with the events recounted and (almost as unanimously) that the names attached to their authorship are inaccurate and belong to the second century. However, if Matthew and Luke make use of Mark, we still have to account for the rest of their contents. That itself falls into two categories. Some of it is shared by the two of them, while the rest is peculiar to Matthew or Luke. The shared material has come to be most widely explained by the hypothesis that there was a separate document or perhaps a fairly standardized oral source, labelled Q, standing for the German *Quelle,* which included (or perhaps consisted of) this material. Mostly it is made up of sayings of Jesus, whether aphorisms or parables or the like. The post-war discovery of the text of the Gospel of Thomas (see Chapter 4) shows that such a work could indeed have existed, though Thomas, while it contains numerous part-parallels to the great Gospels, is certainly not it – mostly breathing an ethos of spiritual writing otherwise unknown in first-century Christian writing (not that this of itself rules it out for an early date, it simply makes it less likely). Such a document would indeed serve plausibly as a primary source for much of the material, largely the teaching of Jesus, otherwise unknown, for Matthew and Luke; but in recent years it has been challenged, especially by some British scholars. Let us suppose, they say, that instead Matthew supplemented Mark and then Luke used both his book and Mark as his primary sources, of course, then adding his own material, derived perhaps from people and places associated with Paul the Apostle, whose devotee he was and whose activities he wrote up in the Acts of the Apostles, his (unique) second volume, written after he had completed his gospel. For technical reasons, this theory makes sense of some of the phenomena of agreements of Matthew and Luke against Mark in the parts of their works that they derived from Mark. Nevertheless, it has to be said that it has not carried wide conviction.

The Gospel of John raises different questions. While certainly identifiable as a Gospel of the same general kind as the others, its content is largely its own, it is much more uniform in style and vocabulary, and it contains a great deal of teaching or hortatory material from Jesus, all in a thoroughly Johannine style, with its relatively narrow key vocabulary, words used time and again (such as 'truth', 'light', 'life'). It also seems to many to have an elevated theological life of its own and its own kind of weight.

But then other interrogations came to be addressed to these books. From what settings did they and their constituent parts arise? Clearly something happened between whatever occurred in the life of Jesus and the writing down, forty to sixty years (it seems) after his time on earth. Surely, stories and teachings were retained (and perhaps created?) in the early Christian communities. True, we have relatively little evidence of this happening – and such as we do have is not encouraging: particularly, the Apostle Paul scarcely ever quotes Jesus' teaching or, still less, refers to incidents in his life (only the Last Supper, 1 Corinthians 11.23–25, and his death and resurrection, 1 Corinthians 15.3–5, the former at least – and encouragingly – appearing in much the same terms as the accounts in the first three Gospels). Of course we do not know what notebooks or memorized material Paul might have had for his own use in teaching – we do not usually put everything we know into letters that have their own special character and purpose; but it does seem probable that his ways of telling of Jesus' importance and meaning did not necessarily lead him to refer to deeds or teachings: he preferred more abstract language, such that most Christians have not found him particularly straightforward from that day to this! And in the two clearest instances of his quoting Jesus' teaching, he chooses not to endorse it – for good reasons relating to his own situation. It is a principle of adaptation that more modern Christians are often less open to following. See 1 Corinthians 7.12 and 9.14.

So let us suppose that the early communities told and re-told stories about Jesus, his marvels and his teachings, and of course crucially the story of his life and especially his death and resurrection. Then: would not these stories have been kept especially if they gave guidance for the belief and practice of the communities themselves, perhaps serving as material for instruction and preaching? And would not the stories have fallen into certain stock forms and acquired more or less fixed ways of being retailed, perhaps memorized? We can even perhaps identify how these stories acquired particular structures, moulded by repetition and standard use.

But then: there is a further step. Does stopping here not reduce the evangelists themselves, whoever they were, to little more than analogous to the subeditors of newspapers, whose task is no more than to arrange and fit together the items they have been given? Should we not suppose that perhaps they were responsible people with ideas of their own: ways of seeing the faith they wrote to propagate, ways of looking at the figure of Jesus, needs to meet in their own communities and ideas about the way those needs ought to be met? They might even have had their own personalities, backgrounds and prejudices that would be likely to express themselves in their writings. And it looks as if, at a lower level in part, they were capable of thinking it important to put things in a particular order, perhaps different from that of a predecessor, and certainly to use their own favourite vocabulary, even considering that of a predecessor as, in some respect or other, barbarous! It is possible to take this perception a long way: one can dignify the evangelists no longer as mere chroniclers, nor even as historians, but as theologians, men of thought, with their own different ways of perceiving the significance of Jesus. And not only as theologians – a prose-bound breed – but men of creative vision: poets indeed.

All this of course seems to remove the Jesus (or the different Jesuses) of the gospels increasingly far from history. How much of these things did he actually do, and how much and what did he actually teach? This thought can be alarming, even vertigo-inducing. But we must get a grip! What alternative can there be, could there have been? We can think back to the beginning of this essay. Of course there is a difference between writing deliberate fiction (such as *The Da Vinci Code*) and retailing in one's own way what one has received – and what can a writer do? Think back to the books about Trafalgar. We can (we believe) now be more efficient about the collection and preserving of evidence than was thought desirable or found possible in former times, and we do hope to know the difference between propaganda and the expression of a legitimate point of view or interpretation of the past. But detached accuracy is a will o'the wisp and objectivity of a total kind is a chimera. And were the evangelists not men with a cause to promote, and were they not bound to commend Jesus in ways helpful to their time and place and audience? Like Paul, their primary concern was to preach Jesus and to convey the 'truth' about him: which they saw as meaning his significance and importance in God's grand design more than fidelity to his precise utterances or his dates or his actions.

So the gospels do not tell us precisely what Jesus said and did, after the manner of a chronicler or conscientious biographer. And if they set out to do that, we might only need one of them – the kind of compendium that people have tried to make out of the four that we have, in the interests of creating a 'life of Jesus': in doing that, of course, they have stifled the voices of all and failed to recognize their individuality – the messages the four of them sought to leave. You have only to read the four narratives of the Passion in the light of what has been said to get the point. Each of them tells much the same story; and we can surely say that the outline is true to history. But each has its own features and its own ethos – indeed, it own doctrine of what is happening here. The easiest way to see this is to examine the sayings of Jesus from the cross as retailed by each evangelist. Mark's comes first and tells us only (15.34): 'My God, my God, why hast thou forsaken me?' It is of course both mysterious and problematic – or on another way of reading it, it is wholly understandable and tragic. Those are possibilities that arise on the assumption that Jesus uttered it. And if he did, then it is a question why Mark saw fit to include such a piece of apparent faithlessness or even blasphemy. But in the context of Mark's whole picture, though it is daring, it may be intelligible. It may be that Mark wishes us to see that Jesus' identification of himself with the human lot, his losing of life in the deepest sense, is his route to achieving his goal: Jesus is living and dying by his own message in 8.34–5. You gain life by losing it, and only so. Luke adopts a quite different view of Jesus' death, this time entirely in accord with the emphases in his presentation of Jesus as the bringer of human good and the reconciler of those at variance; so Jesus says, instead, 'Father, forgive them' (23.34), 'Today you will be with me in paradise' (23.43, to the penitent thief), and 'Father, into thy hands I commend my spirit' (23.46): it is classic Lukan teaching; which does not at all mean that it is faithless to the message of Jesus or the meaning of the Passion. John has his separate trio of sayings: in 19.26–27, the mutual commending of mother and beloved disciple; in 19.28, 'I thirst', where a deeper sense is not clearly identifiable; and 19.30, 'It is finished', meaning that all has been fulfilled and completed, which amply rounds off John's whole sense of Jesus' purposeful arrival and passage in this world, for our salvation and our grasp of the God who, in him, grasps us.

There is one other topic which ought to receive an airing – not because it is central but because it comes up in Dan Brown's novel and is in any case quite a good example of some of the matters we have been considering. It is the special case of Mary Magdalene. Whatever legends grew up about her in later times (see other chapters in this book), the gospels give no support to them. She is simply one of the women in the entourage of Jesus, making only marginal appearances, apart from her role in the context of the stories of the passion and resurrection.

The gospels are not either the first or the last great and influential writings to be both more and less than they seem at first sight. To see them as mere chronicles of (on any showing) just some of the things Jesus did and taught is to miss most of what they have to say. It does scant justice to a writer to fail to grasp his main intention! Not that a writer has a monopoly of his work's future or a control over what people may make of it – but there are also injustices and mistakes. Certainly, there is no other evidence on which people may erect more accurate structures for Jesus' history. Equally certainly, even where we cannot assert accuracy about the details of his life and teaching, some things are so clear that we do well to recognize how powerful they are and to see where they leave us. He was certainly a Jew of his time who gave himself to the service of God's cause, seen in terms then available: the rule of God soon to be manifested in its fullness in overwhelming clarity. He taught his followers ideals of service and self-sacrifice for the cause of God; and he lived out a courageous life of service to the outcasts of his day. He attempted to create new kinds of community, where one sat down to table together with unfamiliar sorts of men and women, transcending the social conventions of the day. He was in that sense counter-cultural. But all for the cause of God, with love as the motive and the keynote – understood without some of the conventions that limited practical application in the society of his day. The effects of his life and his subsequent fate remain with us, some more in character than others – and his followers have done strange things with him, as well as splendid and heroic ones. And we know enough to keep us going very nicely indeed!

Further Reading

J. D. Crossan, *The Historical Jesus* (HarperSanFrancisco, 1991) is a fascinating account of Jesus' thought and behaviour, seeing him as a Galilean, a preacher who had been influenced by the ideas of the Cynics, with an emphasis on common meals and new kinds of social life. A. E. Harvey, *Jesus and the Constraints of History* (Duckworth, 1982) is a first-rate, sober account of Jesus in the setting of the Judaism and the Palestine of his day. In *Jesus, the Complete Guide* (edited by Leslie Houlden, Continuum, 2005), there are some 200 articles dealing with all kinds of aspects of Jesus in history, thought and culture. J. Leslie Houlden, *Jesus, A Question of Identity* (Continuum, 2006) gives a concise account of the different ways in which Jesus has been seen and thought about down the centuries. One of the major contributions to recent attempts to identify Jesus in the context of his day is John P. Meier, *A Marginal Jew* (Doubleday, 1991, 1994). And Mark Allen Powell, *The Jesus Debate* (Lion, 1998) gives a good and reliable guide to the state of recent discussions about the Jesus of history.

Chapter 2
Who Were the Disciples?

Stephen Need

It is quite clear that later Christian tradition says a lot more about the twelve disciples of Jesus than what is found in the New Testament. In the gospels, Jesus calls twelve disciples who accompany him during his ministry in Galilee, who are with him at the Last Supper in Jerusalem, and who are involved in the events that lead to his arrest, trial and crucifixion. But even though there is some information about the disciples there isn't very much, and later Christian writers soon filled in the biographical gaps left by the evangelists. From early on the disciples certainly inspired the Christian imagination. Some of them are already presented in different ways in the four gospels and traditions about them grew and developed significantly in the next few centuries. These traditions were eventually captured in frescoes, mosaics, icons and paintings, and the disciples' names were attached to churches, cathedrals and pilgrim shrines across the world. From the early second century onwards, stories relating to the lives of the disciples took on a vitality of their own and played a very significant role in the development of Christian culture and piety.

Where exactly did the many traditions about the twelve disciples of Jesus come from and how reliable are they? In the decades that followed the writing of the gospels Christians told stories about the disciples to substantiate and defend their faith. These stories have come down to us in a collection of documents known as the 'apocryphal acts' (see Chapter 4). They tell of the lives and travels of the disciples, of their healings and conversions and of their deaths as martyrs. Most of this literature comes from the second and third centuries, and some later, and is almost completely legendary in nature. The early centuries of Christianity were filled with fierce theological controversy and most of the literature that we shall consider here was written in that context. There were already many different strands of Christian belief at the time and the concepts of 'orthodoxy' and 'heresy' were only gradually being thrashed out. Most of the 'apocryphal' literature was eventually considered 'unorthodox' or 'heretical' and was not included in the New

Testament. It is this literature in conjunction with later sources that gives us most of the relevant material on the lives of the disciples.

In this essay, I shall first consider the New Testament evidence for the lives of the disciples; second, discuss some of the traditions about the disciples found in the early Christian 'apocryphal acts' and other sources; and third, look briefly at some relevant archaeological data. I shall conclude that most of the evidence we have for the lives of the disciples is legendary and therefore historically unreliable.

New Testament Evidence

The documents of the New Testament, especially the gospels, written forty to sixty years after the events, constitute the earliest material we have concerning the lives of the disciples of Jesus. The best thing to do is simply to note some of the things they say about the disciples although it must be borne in mind that the details noted here all fall within a particular evangelist's overall portrayal. For example, Mark presents the disciples of Jesus as somewhat dim and constantly failing to understand Jesus' words whereas this feature is toned down by the later evangelists. Also, although details about an individual disciple might be shared by the different gospels, the overall presentation of that disciple in a particular gospel might be different. Thus, Peter's character is improved by successive gospel writers while that of Judas gets worse. It is worth noting that the four lists of disciples' names (Mark 3.16–19; Matthew 10.2–4; Luke 6.14–16; and Acts 1.13) differ in some details and this perhaps already hints at different traditions. The question of whether there really were twelve disciples has often been raised on the grounds that the number might be symbolic of Jesus fulfilling God's promises to the twelve tribes of Israel, though there is no reason why Jesus himself did not have such symbolism in mind. As for the overall historical setting of the disciples' lives in the gospels, it is Galilee and Jerusalem in the first century CE. Some of them come from Capernaum and Bethsaida near the northern end of the Sea of Galilee, a small town and a city in which people made a living from agriculture and fishing.

According to the gospels of Matthew, Mark and Luke, Peter and his brother Andrew were the first disciples to be called to follow Jesus along with another pair of brothers called James and John. They were all called to follow Jesus while at work fishing on the Sea of Galilee (Mark 1.16f).

We begin with Peter, the disciple most frequently mentioned in the gospels and also the most prominent. Peter came from Bethsaida (John 1.44) but had a house in Capernaum (Mark 1.29f). He was also known as Simon and Cephas and was married (1 Corinthians 9.5). He soon became one of an inner group of disciples that was particularly close to Jesus and became the spokesman for the whole group. On one important occasion he called Jesus 'the Christ' and was rebuked by him for rejecting his prophecy of his coming passion (Mark 8.27–30). He was a committed, though vacillating, character who at the time of Jesus' trial in Jerusalem denied that he even knew him (Mark 14.53–72). Overall, the gospels of Matthew and Luke improve Peter's character as portrayed by Mark. Matthew presents him in a more positive light, for example in the Confession at Caesarea Philippi (16.13–20), and a still more positive picture appears in Luke who softens Peter's denials of Jesus (cf. Mark 14.71 with Luke 22.54–62). In John, Peter is second to the 'beloved disciple' (who is never named) throughout the gospel (20.1–10). Peter also plays a key role in Luke's second volume, the Acts of the Apostles (Acts 3.1–10; 10; and 15), and already in the letters of Paul (Galatians 2; 1 Corinthians 1.12). By contrast, Peter's brother Andrew is far less significant in the New Testament. According to John's gospel he was the first disciple to be called (1.35f), had been a disciple of John the Baptist, and came from Bethsaida. Beyond this there is nothing else about him. Many of the differences of presentation are in tune with the overall outlook of the evangelist concerned.

James and John are the other pair of brothers who were among the first disciples to be called. They are the 'sons of Zebedee' (Mark 1.19) and John was probably the younger of the two. They are nicknamed 'Boanerges' or 'sons of thunder' probably on account of their characters (Mark 10.35–37). They seem to have come from a wealthy family as they had hired servants in the boat with them when they were called (Mark 1.20). Along with Peter, they were part of the inner group that was particularly close to Jesus. Some people have thought that this John is the disciple known as the 'beloved disciple' in John's gospel. He also appears in the Acts of the Apostles with Peter but is not as important (Acts 3.1–11; 4.1–22; 8.14–25). According to Acts 12. If James suffered martyrdom under Herod Agrippa in Jerusalem and is the only one of the twelve whose martyrdom is known in the New Testament. This James is sometimes known as 'James the Great'.

Probably the best known of Jesus' twelve disciples is Judas Iscariot. He is known to most people for 'betraying' Jesus. He is also the best

example of a disciple whose image changed even across the pages of
the New Testament and around whom a number of different traditions
developed very early on. The first thing to note about him is his name:
Judas Iscariot. What does the 'Iscariot' mean? Does it come from the
Hebrew *ish* and *kerioth* meaning 'the man from Kerioth'? Or is it somehow connected to the word 'sicarii'? The 'sica' was a curved dagger and
the 'Sicarii' were a group of 'dagger bearers' that operated during the
Jewish War against Rome in 66–70 CE. Could Judas have belonged to
an earlier manifestation of such a group? There is no clear answer but
there was a place called Kerioth in southern Judaea and it certainly could
be that Judas came from there. If so, he would be the only non-Galilean
disciple and would have been separated from the others from the beginning. Nothing is made of his home town in the gospels, however, and his
key role lies in the part he plays in Jesus' arrest and death.

Although Judas has been portrayed for centuries as the one who
betrayed Jesus, it is actually unclear from the New Testament that,
historically, this is quite the way to put it. In the Gospel of Mark he is
a more innocent figure than in the other three gospels. All of the twelve
fail in the crisis of the death of Jesus, as indeed earlier in the Gospel,
and Mark gives us no reason to suppose that he does not share in the
restoration indicated in Mark 16.7: for Mark, all are sinners and all are
to be redeemed. Matthew, with his concern for people receiving their just
deserts (16.27 etc.), emphasizes the sordid matter of Judas betraying for
money (26.14, 16), and though he tells of Judas' later remorse, he shows
how Judas certainly meets a terrible end (27.3–10). Luke calls Judas
by the term 'traitor' (6.16), but he softens the manner of his death –
it is a nasty accident rather than any kind of vengeance from above
(Acts 1.16–20) – and see below concerning later developments (p.25f).
John increases the demonizing of Judas. 6.70; 13.2, 10–11.

It is worth noting that the word commonly translated 'betray' in fact
nowhere in Greek literature means any more than 'hand over', though
of course it can in particular contexts carry further connotations. But in
essence, for Mark at the beginning of the telling of the story, Judas was
the informer who tells the authorities where Jesus is to be found. Jesus
did not prevent the carrying out of the arrangement.

There is some confusion over the figure of Matthew – going back
almost to the beginning. In Mark there is a story of the call of Levi, a
tax-collector (2.13). In Matthew the figure concerned is called 'Matthew'.
Now this evangelist has a tidy mind, and it may be that he was uneasy that

this quite prominent story of the call of a disciple related to someone who does not appear in the list of the twelve in Mark 3.16–19, and so he made good the deficiency. (Note that the attribution of the first gospel to Matthew is a second-century addition.) Luke, it appears, was content with 'Levi' as he found it in Mark (5.27–31), and indeed lengthened the story with a feast given by Levi, a kind of farewell party. It may of course be that older legends are true: that the man concerned had two names! In any case, nothing more is known about him. Nor is there much to be said about the rest of the twelve. There is, however, Thomas. We only learn much about him from the Gospel of John. He is nicknamed 'Didymus', 'the twin', the name 'Thomas' itself meaning 'twin' in Aramaic. Thomas is present at the raising of Lazarus (John 11.16) and at the Resurrection of Jesus when he says that he will not believe that Jesus has risen unless he can see him and put his finger in the mark of the nails. When he finally sees Jesus and is invited to do so, he confesses 'My Lord and my God' (John 20.26–29). Because he was not prepared to believe until he had seen the risen Jesus he became known as the 'doubting Thomas' and gave rise to this expression.

The rest of the twelve remain almost faceless in the New Testament but as we shall see this did not mean that they had no future ahead of them! One of the disciples about whom we know least is Philip. In the first three gospels he is mentioned only in the lists of disciples. In John's Gospel he is said to come from Bethsaida (John 1.45–46; 12.21); brings Nathanael (perhaps to be identified with Bartholomew?) to Christ; and is present at the feeding of the five thousand (6.5–7). When some Greeks want to see Jesus, Philip is mentioned (12.20–26) and he is the one who asks Jesus to show the disciples the Father (14.8). There have been differences of opinion across the centuries concerning the relation between Philip the disciple and the Philip of Acts 8.26–40. We know even less about Bartholomew. His name might come from 'Bar Tholmai' which in Aramaic means 'the son of Tholmai'. His first name could have been Nathanael and he would then have been 'Nathanael Bar Tholmai' or Nathanael the son of Tholmai. Because Bartholomew is not mentioned in John's Gospel and a disciple called Nathanael is mentioned there but not in the other gospels, it came to be thought that Bartholomew and Nathanael are the same person. In the synoptic gospels Bartholomew and Philip are linked and in John's Gospel Nathanael and Philip are linked. Nathanael came from Cana in Galilee (John 21.2).

Hardly anything is known about James the Son of Alphaeus, Simon the Zealot and Jude. There are up to seven people called James in the New

Testament including James the brother of Jesus (Mark 6.3) who later becomes a leader in the Jerusalem Church (Acts 15.13) and who according to Eusebius' *Ecclesiastical History* became the first Bishop of Jerusalem. It was James the brother of Jesus whose ossuary or bone box was said to have been found in Jerusalem a few years ago but which turned out to be a forgery. However, this James was not one of the twelve disciples.

From all this, it can be seen that the gospel portraits of the disciples are sketchy and incomplete. It can also be seen that there are different interpretations of the disciples' characters and significance across the four gospels. Each evangelist paints his own picture and although these have much in common there are also significant differences. This raises the fundamental question of the historical reliability of the gospel narratives but the New Testament writers' concern is not simply to provide historical information about the disciples. They portray these men in relation to their own overall understanding of Jesus to whom the disciples are always secondary. We cannot, therefore, be confident about the historical reliability of every detail. But in later centuries a range of colourful traditions developed out of the gospel sketches and formed the basis of a genre of literature known as the 'apocryphal acts'. It is this literature that preserves most of the later legends about the lives of the disciples.

Apocryphal Acts and Other Sources

In this section, the focus will be on the so-called 'apocryphal acts'. The word 'apocryphal' means 'hidden' and refers to early Christian books that were not incorporated into the New Testament. They are narratives that tell of the lives, activities and deaths of the disciples and they fill in the biographical gaps left by the New Testament writers. This literature is mostly from the second and third centuries, though some is later, and contains legendary and imaginary material. There are quite a lot of 'apocryphal acts' including the *Acts of Peter*, the *Acts of John*, the *Acts of Thomas* and the *Acts of Philip* (see Chapter 4). There is also an enormous amount of other apocryphal literature that should be mentioned here such as gospels, epistles and apocalypses. For example, the *Gospel of Thomas* has become widely known as one of the 'gnostic gospels' discovered at Nag Hammadi in Egypt in 1945; the *Gospel of Mary Magdalene* is now well known because of what it may say about Jesus' relationship with Mary Magdalene; and the *Gospel of Judas* has recently received a great deal of attention giving evidence of a reassessment of Judas' character by some Christians by the third century. Other material includes works such as the *Epistle of Barnabas* and the *Apocalypse of Paul*. All this material was written in the context of controversy between various early Christian groups, especially between those known as 'gnostics' (seeking secret *gnosis* or knowledge) and those that later became 'orthodox' (having right opinion or belief). All these texts are part of the same body of apocryphal literature and their discovery in recent decades has helped us understand more about the complexity of early Christianity. However, hardly any of this material is historically reliable.

One other question should be raised before looking at the 'apocryphal acts' themselves: who wrote them? The short answer is that they are anonymous. It is important to note that books in the ancient world were sometimes written anonymously, for example the four New Testament gospels: Matthew, Mark, Luke and John. We do not know who the authors were and the four names that are so well known today were, it seems, added in the second century. Other books in the ancient world were written under a false name, for example some of the New Testament epistles that claim to be by Peter or Paul: 1 and 2 Peter claim to be by Peter but are most likely not, while 1 and 2 Timothy and Titus claim to be by Paul but are most likely not. The practice of writing under another name is known as 'pseudonymity' and was intended to give a work a degree of authority that it might not otherwise have. Some of the apocryphal literature is written under false names particularly apocryphal gospels such as the *Gospel of Philip* and the *Gospel of Mary Magdalene*. According to some scholars these must be seen as forgeries. Today, the practice seems deplorable. In the period, however, it seems that writers sought to promote a particular line of devotion or belief by claiming the patronage of an appropriate hero of the Christian past, such as Peter or Paul: 'he would have said this if he were here'. The 'apocryphal acts', however, do not claim to be by anyone. It has been thought in the past that they were all written by the same author but the usual view today is that even though they have much in common in style and content they were most probably written by different authors. In any case their subject matter gave them all the authority they needed in the eyes of those for whom they were written.

We begin with the late second-century *Acts of Peter* in which Peter travels to Rome by boat during the reign of the Emperor Nero (54–68 CE), and converts the Captain on the way. Christ has asked him to go to Rome to counter the teaching of Simon Magus (with whom Peter is in conflict in the Acts of the Apostles 8.9–24). Peter does this and is soon involved preaching, healing and raising the dead. There is significant opposition to Peter in Rome and he eventually decides to leave the city. On his way out he meets Christ and asks him 'Lord, where are you going?' (*Domine, quo vadis?*). Jesus tells him that he is going back to Rome to be re-crucified. Peter realizes that he should go back to the city and face death with his Lord. He is eventually arrested and put to death hanging upside-down on a cross in Rome. He preaches a long sermon from the cross explaining the significance of his death. The tradition of Peter's tomb in Rome (discussed in the next section) is known from the second century. By the fourth century Peter had become a key figure in the ministry and leadership of the western church, symbolizing authority based at Rome. In due course he was seen as the first Pope and all subsequent Popes were then seen as successors to him.

In the second- or third-century *Acts of Andrew* Peter's brother, Andrew travels widely and ends up in Patras in Greece. He preaches the gospel, and converts and heals people through which he alienates the Governor and is eventually condemned to death by crucifixion. His tomb is still marked in Patras today. The tradition that he was crucified on an X-shaped cross arose later from the idea that he was not worthy to die on a cross exactly like Jesus, probably the same reason that Peter was said to have died on an upside down cross in Rome. The X-shaped cross became known as 'St. Andrew's cross' and Andrew later became patron saint of Greece. In the fourth century St. Jerome said that Andrew's bones were taken to Constantinople. In an eighth-century tradition, an angel told a monk called Regulus to take some of Andrew's bones west from Constantinople. Regulus eventually found himself on the east coast of Scotland where he founded St. Andrews and became its first bishop! Andrew then became patron saint of Scotland. Because of travels in Scythia in Russia he also later became patron saint of Russia.

James and John played an important part in later Christian tradition and major places of Christian pilgrimage developed in association with them: *Santiago de Compostela* in Spain, and Ephesus (now in Turkey). In Eusebius' *Ecclesiastical History* he claims that in the second century Clement of Alexandria said that when James was beheaded, one of his accusers was converted, taken away and beheaded with James. In a sixth- or seventh-century work known as the *Apostolic History* of Pseudo-Abdias James gets involved with two magicians called

Hermogenes and Philetus. Philetus is converted by James and tells Hermogenes to disappear. Hermogenes gets angry and puts Philetus under a magical spell, but James sends his kerchief to Philetus and he is released from the spell. Eventually, after a struggle with devils, Hermogenes is converted and does miracles himself. The story of James's travels continues after his death. According to Isidore of Seville in Spain in the seventh century, the two magicians put James's body in a lead coffin and set sail with it. The next day they find themselves on the coast of Spain. James's body rests at a place called Iria Flavia where many miracles are associated with it. The body gets lost in the eighth-century but is re-discovered in the ninth and taken to Compostela by the King of Spain. The name *Santiago de Compostela* is probably a Spanish corruption of the Latin for 'St. James the Apostle'.

The late second-century *Acts of John* tells of John going to Ephesus in Asia Minor as the result of a vision. He arrives in the city, performs miracles, heals the sick and raises the dead. He even destroys the Temple of Artemis. After travelling to nearby Smyrna and other places in Asia Minor he returns to Ephesus where a grave is eventually dug for him and he lies down and dies. The Ephesus tradition is usually linked up with the claim that it was this John who wrote the New Testament Gospel of John, the three Letters of John and the Book of Revelation. It is thought that John was exiled to the island of Patmos where he wrote Revelation and then went to Ephesus where he wrote the gospel and the letters. The tradition of John at Ephesus is known to Eusebius in the fourth century but is unknown to significant writers in the early second century and its authenticity is disputed by many today. Perhaps there were a number of Johns that were gradually merged into one?

As in the New Testament, Judas turns out to be one of the most interesting disciples in later tradition. His image changes and develops and he is the focus of many stories and interpretations. In *The Arabic Infancy Gospel*, a work of uncertain date, Judas is possessed by the devil in infancy and is known thereafter as demonic. There is also a more positive tradition about Judas, for example in the second-century *Gospel of Judas*, which has received recent attention in the media. In this tradition, Judas is seen as a friend of Jesus and as one who played the key role in God's plan of salvation. This more positive outlook on this disciple reappears in the 1970s musical *Jesus Christ Superstar*. In spite of the mixed tradition, however, the portrayal of Judas has been largely negative: he was an evil if necessary part of God's purposes. Over the centuries he became the epitome of betrayal and rejection, a symbol of evil, the archetypal Jew who rejected the messiah, and a typical pathetic human being who betrayed God and his fellow-men.

In the third-century *Acts of Andrew and Matthew* (sometimes *Matthias*) and the *Martyrdom of Matthew*, Matthew travels to the 'land of the cannibals' and is captured by them to be eaten. The apostle Andrew goes by boat to try to rescue him and there is a storm at sea. All turns out well, however, when Andrew realizes that the boat is being rowed by Jesus. Later, Andrew gets imprisoned but eventually preaches to the cannibals and Matthew is freed. In the second text, Matthew goes back to the land of the cannibals to preach to them but they burn him alive. There are many other later traditions relating to Matthew's life. For example Eusebius says that Matthew preached the gospel in Judaea and wrote a gospel in Hebrew that was eventually translated into Greek. The Hebrew gospel was then taken to India. This Matthew was thought to be the author of the Gospel of Matthew in the New Testament but there is no other evidence of any of this.

Thomas has received a great deal of attention in recent years because of the Coptic *Gospel of Thomas*. However, it is the third-century *Acts of Thomas* that has this disciple travelling to India to preach the gospel. This tradition gave rise to the 'Thomas Christians' who still exist in India today. In the text, the disciples cast lots in order to see which country each shall go to and India falls to Thomas. A merchant called Abban sent by the Indian King Gundaphorus appears and takes Thomas with him to India. Thomas is asked to build a palace for the King but then in the King's absence gives the money he has received for this purpose to the poor and so builds a 'heavenly city'. Through this action he converts the King and his brother to Christianity. Thomas travels around India preaching to the poor, healing the sick, casting out demons and raising the dead. He is assisted by wild asses and challenges all manner of sin and depravity including adultery and carnal pleasure. The crowds follow him, listen to his message about Jesus and are converted; they even see him as a god. Thomas is portrayed as the twin brother of Jesus and as a carpenter. After several spells in prison, he is eventually condemned to death. He is taken into the mountains by four soldiers who spear him to death and bury him. Subsequently, when the king's son is ill and the king wants a miracle from Thomas's bones, he finds the apostle's body gone. According to another tradition it was transported to Edessa in Syria. The whole story of Thomas's journey to India has been treated with the utmost seriousness by many scholars because the names of the characters involved are names of real historical individuals. However, the literature is clearly riddled with legend, of a pattern now familiar, and many now treat it with total scepticism.

Philip is also known because of a gospel named after him. The *Gospel of Philip* contains material relating to Jesus and Mary Magdalene. It is the fourth- or fifth-century *Acts of Philip*, however, that tells us about Philip himself. In this work, lots are cast and Philip is sent to Greece. Like the other disciples, he preaches, heals people and raises the dead. Eventually he arrives at Hierapolis in Asia Minor. Bartholomew is with him and John joins him later. Eventually Philip is arrested and hanged upside down after having his ankles and thighs pierced. Philip calls for a chasm to open up and swallow all his opponents but Jesus appears and tells him that he should not have done this. As a punishment he tells Philip that he will have to wait outside heaven for forty days before entering. Philip finally dies and is buried in Hierapolis. As in the New Testament, Philip is linked with Bartholomew in later tradition. Bartholomew is present with Philip in Asia Minor and in the *Martyrdom of Bartholomew* dies by being put into a bag and dropped into the sea.

Finally, there is no significant later evidence of James the Son of Alphaeus and Simon the Zealot. There is a Letter of Jude in the New Testament that some scholars have thought was written by Jude the disciple but others think it was written later under Jude's name to give it authority. Eusebius of Caesarea cites the second-century Heggesipus as saying that some grandsons of Jude were accused of being related to David and to Jesus and were brought before the Emperor Domitian to be punished. They were later perceived not to be a threat and were released. This implies that there were blood relatives of Jesus around in the second century and that Jude was still known as having been a brother of Jesus. Jude's fate is tied up with Simon the Zealot's in the *Apostolic History* of Pseudo Abdias in which they go to Persia and are martyred.

From the 'apocryphal acts' and other literature it can be seen that there exists a rich and fascinating collection of traditions that tell of the lives and deaths of the disciples of Jesus. These traditions grew up first during centuries of controversy and after the fourth century during an age in which Christianity flourished. The disciples of Jesus had gradually become idealized examples of Christian faith and were held up as heroes and even as gods. In the end, however, the 'apocryphal acts' and later sources tell us more about the growth of Christianity during the early centuries than about the lives of the disciples themselves. They are later than the times in which they are set and are largely legendary in character. They cannot therefore be taken seriously as historical evidence.

Archaeological Data

Archaeological data play a minor role where historical evidence for the lives of the disciples is concerned but a few things are worth mentioning. The prevalence of Peter in early Christianity led to two major pilgrimage centres of which there are some remains today. First, Peter's tomb in Rome: this was known from the second century and pilgrims soon started to visit it. By the fourth century, Eusebius of Caesarea knew of the tradition of Peter's death in Rome and Constantine the Great, the first Christian Emperor, built a basilica over the alleged site of the tomb. This church was rebuilt centuries later and is now St. Peter's Basilica at the Vatican. When Pope Pius XI died in 1939 and preparation began for his burial, tombs and bones were discovered under St. Peter's. Some archaeologists believed that the tomb and bones of Peter himself had been found although this is still widely disputed today. Second, 'Peter's House' in ancient Capernaum near the Sea of Galilee: the remains of a pilgrimage church from the fifth century have been found in a series of excavations beginning in the nineteenth century. This church was built over a second-century house church made out of a first-century residence thought to be Peter's house. Peter's House is now visited frequently by pilgrims to the Holy Land but again there is much debate about its authenticity.

Another important pilgrimage centre of the sixth century was the Basilica of St. John in Ephesus. Following the growth of the tradition that John the disciple went to Ephesus, wrote a gospel and died there, the Emperor Justinian built a basilica over the reputed site of John's grave. This soon became the focus of a 'cult of John' and pilgrims travelled from far and wide. The church was destroyed in the fourteenth century, most likely by an earthquake. It has now been excavated and partly reconstructed. A church was also built in Hierapolis in the early Byzantine period marking the grave of Philip. Finally, a living pilgrim centre functions in Spain at *Santiago de Compostela* where it is claimed that the body of James the Great still lies under the Cathedral of St. James. This has continued to be an important place of pilgrimage since the ninth century.

In spite of its significance in later centuries, none of the archaeological material noted here provides any evidence for the lives of the disciples themselves. It speaks only of the flowering of later traditions associated with them, and of the beginning of the cult of saints which became such a big feature of Christian devotion.

Conclusion

In conclusion, it can be seen that later Christian tradition filled out the sketchy portrayals of the twelve disciples of Jesus found in the New Testament. The four gospels do provide some details but not many and certainly not of the sort that really count as historical evidence. In some cases, disciples are presented differently across the several gospels and are 'painted up' in the context of the evangelists' individual outlooks and theologies. It is difficult, therefore, to get a sense from the gospels of who these men really were as historical figures. The gaps left by the gospel writers were filled in later largely by the authors of the so-called 'apocryphal acts', a series of texts mostly from the second and third centuries that tell of the disciples' travels to different countries; their miraculous healings and conversions; and their dramatic deaths as martyrs. The early Christians wrote these narratives at times of serious controversy in the early centuries of Christianity when the disciples had become idealized models of Christian faith. There is also other later literature that continued to develop the traditions. In general it is clear that the 'apocryphal acts' and the later literature, and the churches and shrines associated with the disciples all tell us more about the expansion of Christianity and the controversies and developments of the early centuries than they do about the disciples themselves. Finally therefore, even though the material that we possess about the lives of the disciples of Jesus constitutes a very important part of Christian tradition, the evidence of the New Testament, the apocryphal acts and later literature, and the archaeological data leave us with a very shadowy sense of who the disciples of Jesus really were.

Further Reading

A good place to begin finding out more about the disciples is with articles on individual disciples in David Noel Freedman (ed.), *The Anchor Bible Dictionary* (Doubleday, 1992, six volumes). These give very useful overviews of everything that is known about each disciple from the New Testament. The texts of the Apocryphal Acts are available in

J. K. Elliott, *The Apocryphal New Testament: A Collection of Apocryphal Christian Literature in an English Translation based on M. R. James* (Oxford University Press, 2005). This very comprehensive volume includes all the main apocryphal texts in an up to date English translation. Many of the traditions about the disciples discussed in this chapter can be found in Elliott. See also G. A. Williamson and A. Louth, *Eusebius: The History of the Church* (Penguin, second edition, 1989) for other traditions about the disciples.

For a recent scholarly discussion of Christianity and its scriptures in the early centuries see Bart D. Ehrman, *Lost Christianities: The Battles for Scripture and the Faiths We Never Knew* (Oxford University Press, 2003). For a full discussion of Judas and his 'betrayal' of Jesus see William Klassen, *Judas. Betrayer or Friend of Jesus?* (SCM, 1996). For detailed discussions of Peter and John and their places in the New Testament and later Christian literature and tradition see Pheme Perkins, *Peter: Apostle for the Whole Church* (T & T Clark, 2000) and Alan R. Culpepper, *John the Son of Zebedee: The Life of a Legend* (T & T Clark, 2000).

Chapter 3
Who Were the First Popes?

Graham Gould

For over a thousand years, from the early Middle Ages until well into modern times, the Papacy was the most important single factor in the history of Christianity. The Popes' claim to possess authority over all Christians shaped the development of the Western church and was central to the way in which relations between Eastern Orthodox and Western Christianity developed following the schism between them in the eleventh century. The rejection of the papal claim was (along with the reform of Catholic doctrine) the main cause of the Protestant Reformation of sixteenth-century Europe, which led in turn to the development of the complex array of competing denominations which characterizes Christianity in the modern world. The Papacy, though regarded by Roman Catholic Christians as a symbol of unity and source of authority, thus became a cause of division and an object of hatred. But during the twentieth century a greater degree of understanding and cooperation among Christians encouraged a more positive attitude to the Papacy among non-Roman Catholics in the West. An ecumenical role for the Pope as a spiritual leader and spokesman for Christianity in the arena of world politics has come to be much more widely acknowledged than would have been imaginable a century ago. This was particularly evident in the early years of the pontificate of Pope John Paul II (elected 1978) and in the widespread hope that his successor Benedict XVI, elected in 2005, should prove willing to continue John Paul's work of ecumenical and international outreach, rather than (as some feared) becoming a more isolationist Pope concerned only with maintaining the internal authority-structures and doctrinal integrity of the Catholic church.

Given the high profile of the Papacy among present-day Christians and in the media, it is understandable that interest should be expressed in the early history of the Papacy and the position which it occupied in the formative centuries of Christian doctrinal and institutional development. Some interpretations attribute to the early Papacy an authoritarian manipulation of the Christian message in the interests of its own power and the suppression of alternative Christianities such as those represented by the gnostic gospels. The picture that emerges from the study of the earliest sources for the development of the Papacy, however, is very different from this view. Evidence for belief in the importance of Rome as a church of apostolic foundation there certainly is; but evidence for the existence of a Papacy exercising authority over other churches or determining the course of doctrinal development is much more difficult to come by. Only after the conversion of Constantine in AD 312 do we find any evidence for the development of a Papacy, in the sense in which later Christians have understood the term; and, even then, the change in the status of the Bishop of Rome was not immediate but gradual and required several centuries to complete. Though not intended to be a complete survey, this chapter will discuss some of the historical evidence, mainly from the pre-Constantinian period, on which this judgement is based.

To begin with, the character of the church in Rome needs to be considered as it appears from the earliest post-New Testament sources, around the year 100. Though Rome was the largest city and capital of the Roman empire, its Christian community was made up largely of Greek-speaking immigrants from elsewhere in the Roman world (not until into the third century are the writings of Roman Christians in Latin, rather than Greek). Because of the size of the city, the Christian community probably consisted of a number of different groups of distinct backgrounds, some Jewish, some gentile. (Paul's letter to the Romans, dating from the 50s of the first century, points to such a situation with its attendant difficulties.) As in other cities, Roman Christians met for worship and teaching in private houses and the church did not possess in its own right any buildings, land, wealth, or a professional leadership. Even if someone with the title of Bishop of Rome existed around the year 100 (which is doubtful), he was not the head of a large organization but probably the leader of a house-church, at the most regarded by other Christian groups within the city as their overall figurehead, but with no power to determine what Christians beyond his own group thought or how they worshipped. Such a person may be the author behind an anonymous letter which has been known since later in the second century as the *First Letter of Clement* because it came to be attributed to the Clement who was regarded as Rome's third bishop following the foundation of the episcopate by Peter (see below). The letter was written on behalf of the Roman church to the church in Corinth; part of its purpose was to encourage the Corinthian Christians to be obedient to the leaders whom the apostles and their successors had appointed. These leaders the letter describes as 'bishops and deacons' (ch.42) or, using a less traditional translation, 'overseers and servants', which strongly implies that at this time neither the Roman nor the Corinthian church possessed just one bishop but a collective leadership, even if one person was appointed to speak or write on behalf of the community.

Other writings from shortly after the year 100 show that the leadership of the churches was not just invested in men with titles such as bishop or deacon: prophets also played an important leadership-role. The teaching of a Roman prophet of the early second century is preserved in a writing called the *Shepherd* of Hermas. Nothing in this work suggests that the Roman church was as yet organized under the leadership of a single bishop; leadership seems to be vested in a number of presbyters (i.e. 'elders' – traditionally translated as 'priests' and probably at this early period still largely synonymous with 'bishops'). A man called Clement is singled out as having a responsibility to send Hermas's teachings to other churches (precisely the function implied by the letter referred to above, if it is correctly attributed to Clement). Whether this implies that Clement exercised a more general leadership is hard to say; but the conclusion that there was no one bishop in Rome in Clement's time or for some years afterwards is also supported by the writings of Ignatius of Antioch (an early martyr for the Christian faith), who does not mention a bishop in his letter to the Roman church, though he refers frequently to bishops in his letters to other cities and indeed stresses that obedience is owed to just one bishop in each church. The correct conclusion to be drawn from this evidence is probably that the speed at which an episcopal form of church government was established varied considerably from city to city, with Rome not leading but lagging somewhat behind other important centres of Christianity. This is readily explicable if the size of Rome and the diverse character of the Christian groups in the city is kept in mind.

How long this situation lasted can be clarified to some extent from later evidence. Towards the end of the second century the theologian Irenaeus of Lyons wrote about the Roman church in his anti-gnostic work *Against Heresies*. He uses the succession of bishops in Rome as an argument that the teaching of the apostles has been preserved intact by the church against the false and constantly changing views of the various gnostic groups. He writes that following Peter and Paul the apostles who founded and organized the Roman church, twelve bishops have succeeded: Linus, Anacletus, Clement (Irenaeus mentions the letter), Evarestus, Alexander, Sixtus, Telesphorus, Hyginus, Pius, Anicetus, Soter, and Eleutherus, the last being bishop at the time of writing. Irenaeus forgets that Christians lived in Rome before either Peter or Paul went there – if indeed the tradition that they did so is reliable; but his evidence is an important starting-point for the later development of the belief that the office of Pope derives its authority from Peter through the unbroken succession of bishops. But it should be noted that, in contrast to later papal theory, Irenaeus does not describe Peter himself as a bishop, and treats Peter and Paul together rather than Peter alone as the founders of the episcopal succession.

By the time Irenaeus wrote the position of bishop must have been an established one, or he could not have appealed to Rome as an example of a succession of apostolically orthodox teachers of the faith. The earlier part of his list, however, reflects the assumption of Irenaeus and his contemporaries that such a position had always existed rather than the reality of the earlier second century. As we have seen, earlier documents do not attest the idea that a Bishop of Rome existed at the time of Clement, and practically nothing is known about the others whom Irenaeus lists before Soter (whose dates can be estimated as *c*.166–174). Christian writings which refer to Rome in this period do not suggest that the situation had changed much since the beginning of the century: it is impossible, for example, to find any evidence for a Bishop of Rome in the writings of the Christian philosopher Justin Martyr, who died in Rome *c*.165. Justin refers to the leader of Christian worship as 'the one who presides'; it is sometimes argued that in his usage this term is synonymous with bishop (as it is in some other early Christian documents), but it could equally well describe the less formal leadership of a house-church.

Irenaeus himself probably knew little about the early names on his list (he may in any case have borrowed it from a slightly earlier writer) and would not have been aware that the office of bishop had developed gradually, reaching a new stage, sufficiently advanced to enable a single bishop to be treated as the leader of the Roman church, only at some point in the later second century. Soter does seem to be the first Roman bishop to be referred to as such by a contemporary, Dionysius, Bishop of Corinth, in a letter praising the generosity of the Roman church towards other Christians in need. (This letter, like much of the surviving evidence for the history of the pre-Constantinian church, is preserved because it was quoted by Eusebius of Caesarea in his *Ecclesiastical History*, completed early in the fourth century: see Eusebius, bk.4, ch.23.)

Irenaeus has more to say about the Roman church. Before introducing the list of bishops he writes as follows in a passage which has attracted a great deal of discussion among scholars:

> For it is necessary that every church, that is, the faithful everywhere, should, on account of its pre-eminent authority, agree with this [Roman] church, in so far as by them [the faithful] everywhere the tradition which is from the apostles is always preserved.
> *Against Heresies*, bk.3, ch.3

The Latin is difficult to translate (Irenaeus wrote in Greek, but most of his work survives only in an early Latin translation), but it seems to mean that Christians throughout the world will prove that they possess the genuine apostolic faith by agreeing with the Roman church (whose authority in matters of faith is assured by the apostles Peter and Paul and the succession of bishops). For some commentators this statement provides an early and clear endorsement of the doctrine of Roman primacy as it developed in subsequent centuries; for others it should not be over-interpreted but seen as a natural comment by an author whose main concern is to defend the embryonic notion of apostolic tradition against gnostic alternatives. Rome is, for Irenaeus, in a sense only the most important *example* (because it was the leading city of the West) of a church which has preserved the apostolic tradition intact; he certainly did not believe that the authority of which he speaks conferred on the Roman church any right to direct the affairs of churches elsewhere.

In the years after Irenaeus wrote *Against Heresies* a little more evidence for the role of the Bishop of Rome begins to emerge, much of it preserved in the *History* of Eusebius. Eleutherus's successor as bishop, Victor (*c.*189–198) is the first (unless we include Clement's letter) whom we know to have tried to influence the churches outside Rome. He did so during a controversy over the proper day for the celebration of the Pascha (the annual commemoration of Jesus' death and resurrection) in relation to the Jewish calendar which early Christians adopted. According to Eusebius (bk.5, ch.24), the bishops of Asia Minor wrote to Victor to defend their practice, derived (they say) from the apostles, of observing the Pascha on the day on which the lambs for the Jewish Passover meal were killed; the alternative, Eusebius claims, of celebrating it only on a Sunday (the day of the resurrection) had been approved by most of the churches. (The full details of the controversy and the evidence as to which practice really was the more ancient are too complex to go into here.)

Victor's response was to attack the Asian bishops in letters and to break off relations with them, presumably in an attempt to make them change their mind. But Eusebius tells us that other bishops did not approve of Victor's action and quotes with approval a letter from Irenaeus to Victor which claims that earlier Roman bishops tolerated the Asian dating of the Pascha even though their own practice was different. (Here, writing some years after *Against Heresies*, Irenaeus provides us with a few extra scraps of information, especially about Bishop Anicetus). It is not known what effect the disagreement between Victor and the Asian bishops had on relations between them over the next few years; but clearly Irenaeus, and following him Eusebius, took the view that local or regional liturgical traditions of ancient origin, even if incompatible, could be accommodated within one (universal) church. This was a view which the development of papal authority in the West was to threaten as the centuries wore on, but in the early church it was by far the more normal opinion.

Though the office of the Roman bishop was developing during this period, it would be wrong to imagine that Victor and his immediate successors now headed something that would be recognizable to us as a modern church. This was far from the case. Christians made up a very small proportion of the population of the Roman empire and individual city churches still resembled private clubs rather than public bodies. While Christianity was beginning to develop distinctive practices in relation to baptism and funeral rites (and churches had started to own cemeteries), worship in general was still simple, without elaborate ceremonial, special vestments for clergy, or designated buildings. Clergy were still probably unpaid and the distinction between ordained leadership and lay followers was not nearly so obvious as it has been throughout most of the church's subsequent history. A local church might be presided over by a bishop, assisted by a body of presbyters or elders and a number of deacons or servants, but there was no complex administrative bureaucracy within each church and no hierarchy binding different churches together with clear rules to govern their relations. The choice of bishops and clergy seems to have been a matter internal to each church, not the responsibility of bishops from elsewhere, and meetings of bishops to discuss doctrinal issues were only just beginning to be organized (the councils of bishops which met during the controversy over the date of the Pascha were some of the earliest). In these circumstances, the capacity of the Roman bishop to exercise any kind of primacy over other churches was non-existent.

During the late second and early third centuries the Roman church seems to have been prone to internal controversies over doctrine. During the episcopate of Victor and his successor Zephyrinus (c.198–217) we have evidence (again preserved mainly by Eusebius) of a party in the Roman church which rejected the divinity of Jesus. Probably, that is, they believed that Jesus was a man anointed (*christos*) by the Holy Spirit at his baptism and confirmed as the Messiah by the evidence of his miracles, rather than a pre-existent divine being who became incarnate as a man.

According to an anonymous author quoted by Eusebius, some time later (perhaps c.230–250) the leaders of this party, or a revival of it, claimed that the true view (that Jesus was not divine) had been taught by all of the Roman bishops until Victor, but then abandoned by Zephyrinus (Eusebius, bk.5, ch.28). In response, the anonymous author first lists earlier writers whose theological works show (in his opinion) that the view that Jesus was both divine and human was the tradition of the universal church; then he claims that the first leader of the heretical group in Rome, called Theodotus the leatherworker, was in fact excluded from communion (*koinonia* – implying both participation in the eucharist and fellowship more generally) by Victor, thus proving that the later group's claims that Victor had supported their teaching were false.

Later, the same writer states, two followers of Theodotus, one of them another Theodotus, persuaded a confessor (i.e. someone who had suffered for the faith during a period of persecution) called Natalius to join their group and become its bishop. Natalius, however, was warned by a series of visions that he had made a mistake, and eventually repented and returned to the church led by Zephyrinus. This incident supplies the first instance in history of an alternative bishop (in later times often referred to as an 'anti-pope') being appointed as a rival to the established Bishop of Rome; it also supplies what seems to be the first specific evidence for the payment of a salary to a church leader, for Natalius received 150 denarii per month from the heretical group. Finally, the anonymous writer lists some further characteristics of the group, stating that its leaders are keen students of logic, geometry, philosophy, and medicine – which he regards as having corrupted their thinking.

There was further controversy in Rome a few years later in the time of the next bishop, Callistus (217–222). The evidence here comes mainly from an anti-heretical writing by a contemporary who knew Callistus well but whose relationship with him was extremely bitter. Scholars often attribute this writing (which is in Greek: Latin had still not become the normal language of Roman Christians) to Hippolytus, which is the name of a Roman martyr some years later and also of a theologian who was the author of biblical commentaries and other works; but there is no certainty that this theory is correct and it is probably best to treat this too as the work of an anonymous author. His main complaints against Callistus are twofold: that Callistus taught a heretical theology and that he encouraged immoral behaviour by allowing offenders to repent and obtain forgiveness of their sins too easily (*Refutation of All Heresies*, 9.12).

The heresy of which Callistus was accused was that of failing to distinguish clearly between God the Father and his Son Jesus – the heresy known to subsequent heresy-hunters as Sabellianism, after Sabellius, its supposed founder. The anonymous author claims that Callistus taxed him (the author, who was clearly at that time a prominent member of the church) with believing in two Gods because he distinguished Father and Son rather than uniting them as one divine being, and that Callistus first, when assistant to Zephyrinus, encouraged but then later, when he became bishop, hypocritically condemned Sabellius (of whose actual views very little is known). Combining this with the story of the Theodotians and some other fragments of evidence which survive, it is clear that Rome in these decades was a centre of often controversial debate over fundamental Christian beliefs such as the divinity of Jesus. (Further details, however, belong to the history of the doctrine of the Trinity, which is beyond the scope of this chapter.) Irenaeus may have believed that the Roman church had always held to the truth taught by the apostles, but the nature of this truth was now strongly contested, and the views preferred by the Popes did not always prevail over alternatives.

Callistus's offer of easy forgiveness, according to his critic, allowed him to attract to his church people whose sins had been reckoned as more serious by other groups (including the one led by the anonymous critic). He also permitted men to be ordained who had married more than once (often regarded as impermissible in the early church on the basis of 1 Timothy 3.2, 12) and condoned other offences, claiming that Jesus' parable of the weeds (Matthew 13.24–30) and other biblical texts justified allowing sinners to remain in the church. The policy of Callistus is one among several pieces of evidence which suggest that at this period the church was making it somewhat easier for people who had committed serious sins to regain their good standing in the Christian community, which not surprisingly led to objections from some people who wanted to take a stricter line.

What can we conclude from this series of incidents about the character of the Roman church? It would be easy to regard the activities of the Theodotians, of Sabellius, and of Callistus' critic (who is often assumed to have set himself up as another anti-pope) as evidence simply of small-scale sectarian deviations from the mainstream of Roman church life. This, however, is not necessarily how it would have appeared to a contemporary observer. Since, as we have seen, the Christian community in Rome seems to have consisted originally of a number of separate groups of distinct backgrounds, perhaps founded and at first led by the owners of the houses in which they met, there was no guarantee that differences of doctrine and practice would not develop among them. Some of the groups now seen as heretical may have had just as good claims as the orthodox community to historical roots among the different house-churches, and may have been quite large (though the exact size of any church in this period is practically impossible to estimate).

It is interesting in this context that both the evidence for the Theodotians and the anonymous writer's criticism of Callistus give the impression that the various Christian groups had the character of competing philosophical schools. Perhaps schools of disciples, presided over by freelance teachers, some ordained and others lay (such as Justin in the middle of the second century and perhaps also the two Theodoti – hence their need, once they were rejected by Victor, to appoint Natalius as bishop) are a better model for the early history of the Roman church than what we think of as an organized church today, or even a federation of independent churches. Some of the gnostic groups active in Rome (where Valentinus taught a philosophically-influenced gnostic form of Christianity in the 140s) probably also had the same character. The growing authority of the Bishop of Rome in the later second and early third centuries would have threatened the independence of some of these schools, and any attempt to impose closer unity upon them would have exposed any theological diversity which had previously been hidden beneath the surface of a looser association. Seen in this light, the hostility of Callistus's critic may be the response of a threatened house-church or Christian school leader to policies which were proving all too successful in mopping up diversity and imposing a new vision of episcopal leadership on Roman Christians.

Some such account as this seems to make the best sense of the evidence for the earliest development of what later became the Papacy, at least as regards the internal development of the Roman church. As we have seen, evidence for any wider sphere of authority for the Bishop of Rome is largely lacking at this time: it was not the Roman church that decided which groups were now to count as orthodox (the consensus of churches, not Papal power, was what marginalized gnosticism) and other bishops could make their own decisions about what theological views were acceptable without feeling the need to defer to Rome.

The mid-third century, however, sees some new developments which bring us slightly closer to the understanding of the Papacy which has prevailed in subsequent centuries. A good starting point is the evidence of a letter (preserved by Eusebius, bk.6, ch.43) of Bishop Cornelius of Rome (251–253) to Bishop Fabius of Antioch. The context is as follows. In 250 the Roman emperor Decius set in motion the first empire-wide persecution of Christianity (previous examples of action against Christians having been local, or at least limited, in scope). The Bishop of Rome was martyred in January 250 and Cornelius succeeded him after an interval of more than a year during which, because of the persecution, it was not possible for the church to choose a bishop. During the interval Novatian, a theologian whose writings include the first systematic treatise on the doctrine of the Trinity which has survived (and the first writing in Latin by a Roman theologian), seems to have played an important role in administering the Roman church, and when Cornelius was chosen as bishop in 251 Novatian set himself up as a rival bishop, using as a justification the view that Cornelius was wrong to allow Christians who had renounced their faith during the persecution, if penitent, to be readmitted to communion. (Novatianism, defined by its rejection of the readmission of serious sinners to communion, continued to exist as a distinct Christian grouping for nearly two centuries.) Cornelius's tone in his letter to Fabius, in which he describes Novatian's actions, is naturally hostile and contains several possibly false accusations; nonetheless it is revealing for what it says about the procedures for ordaining a bishop and the condition of the Roman church at the time.

Cornelius writes that Novatian invited three Italian bishops to Rome on the pretext of needing their advice in a dispute and, after getting them drunk, persuaded them to ordain him bishop. One of these three had since repented and been readmitted to communion by Cornelius (though as a layman, no longer as a bishop); the other two had been deposed and successors appointed. What we see from this is that by the mid-third century, the participation of other bishops in episcopal ordinations was necessary to validate the choice of candidate and the ordination itself: it was no longer sufficient for a local church independently to choose and ordain its own bishop. Second, we see that the Bishop of Rome now possessed the right to depose and replace bishops elsewhere in Italy whom he disapproved of. Probably both these developments were a natural result of the establishment of new bishoprics in Italy on the initiative of the Roman church as new Christian communities were founded or grew in numbers. These new bishoprics would naturally enjoy a close relationship with Rome, and perhaps gain the right to some (at least informal) say in who occupied the office of Pope. By this process, Rome established its authority over the rest of Italy as its ecclesiastical province. This was not a uniquely Roman development: the same thing was happening elsewhere, in North Africa, where the leading church was Carthage, in Egypt (Alexandria) and in Syria (Antioch); but in the case of Rome it was eventually to prove possible for the Popes to establish authority over a much wider area, the whole of the Western empire, because of Rome's status as the imperial capital and only apostolically founded church of the West.

Cornelius continues with a descriptive passage about the Roman church:

> Thus the vindicator of the gospel [Novatian] was unaware that there can be only one bishop in a Catholic church, in which, as he knew perfectly well, there are forty-six presbyters, seven deacons, seven sub-deacons, forty-two assistants, fifty-two exorcists, readers, and doorkeepers, and more than fifteen hundred widows and distressed persons. All these are supported by the Master's grace and love for men. But this vast community … together with laity too numerous to count, did not suffice to turn him from such a hopeless, crazy ambition and recall him to the church.

The picture that emerges here is quite different from anything available from half a century earlier and is testimony to a period of rapid growth in numbers and in organization. The bishop is now assisted in his oversight of the churches in Rome by a staff of over 150, occupying both the traditional ordained ministries of presbyter and deacon and a range of minor offices. The widows and distressed people mentioned are presumably supported, like at least some of the officials, out of church funds.

As strong episcopal leadership developed in the various provinces of the empire, tensions might develop between them. This is illustrated a few years later by the strained relationship between Cyprian of Carthage (249–258) and Stephen of Rome (254–257). Cyprian had supported Cornelius in his dispute with Novatian, but opposed Stephen over the latter's policy of accepting converts from heretical or schismatic groups of Christians into the Roman church without demanding that they be rebaptized. Cyprian considered that baptisms administered by heretics were invalid and therefore that a new baptism of converts in these circumstances was necessary. The fact that this debate could take place and be held to be of importance shows how many different Christian sects there already were in the third century and how frequent transfers from one to another must have been. While Stephen had the apostolic prestige of the Roman church behind him, Cyprian was supported by nearly a hundred North African bishops meeting in council in Carthage – a fact which underlines how rapidly the administrative mechanisms of the church were developing during this period.

Relations between bishops in the mid-third century are also illustrated by a letter written by Bishop Dionysius of Rome (259–268) to his namesake, Dionysius of Alexandria (247–264). The subject, as in the time of Callistus, is the doctrine of the Trinity, or more precisely, the relationship between God the Father and his Son. Christians in Libya had complained to Dionysius of Rome that Dionysius of Alexandria was teaching that the Son of God, though a divine being, was inferior to the Father. The Pope's response is critical of Dionysius and suggests that his own view, and therefore presumably the official teaching of the Roman church, still, despite the strictures of Callistus's anonymous critic, leant towards the position of Callistus and Sabellius, who had emphasized the unity of Father and Son. (The theological issues are, however, complex, and this summary does not do justice to their subtlety: it would be anachronistic to regard the views of either Dionysius as heretical, since we do not know how they would have reacted to the debates which resulted in the Creed of Nicaea just over 60 years later.) What we see here is an early example of a Bishop of Rome seeking to act as the guardian of orthodoxy for the whole church, with a duty to correct other bishops – even other regional leaders such as the Bishop of Alexandria. But as yet there was no formal system of canon law, church courts, or process of denunciation, trial, or appeal by which such a papal function could be carried out; only the means of fraternal correction by letter and debate.

By the beginning of the fourth century the Bishops of Rome had certainly become important figures in the church, with some authority over the churches in Italy and high prestige elsewhere. Quite probably, the Roman bishop was regarded by many as the senior bishop of the church because of the status of the capital city and its association with the leading apostles. From this time on, there is much more evidence for the activities of the Roman bishops and for the gradual extension of their authority, particularly within the Western church, and it is impossible in the context of a brief chapter to continue to trace the development in any detail. When the Emperor Constantine became a Christian it was clearly natural for him to treat the Bishop of Rome as an important figure and we find successive bishops, Miltiades (311–314) and Silvester (314–335) involved in the condemnation of the Donatist schism (a dispute within the North African churches which had arisen during the Great Persecution begun by the Emperor Diocletian in 303); this marked an important stage in the process by which both the Emperor and the Pope came to play a role in the doctrinal and disciplinary decisions of the church.

During the doctrinal controversies of the fourth century, which began in Alexandria with the teaching of Arius, it was equally natural for bishops, particularly in the West, to look to Rome for leadership, and for Eastern bishops, seeking support, to wish to remain on good terms with the Bishops of Rome. Nonetheless, it is important not to exaggerate the influence of the Popes on doctrinal decisions made during this period. Papal influence on the Council of Nicaea of 325 was minimal compared with the influence of the Emperor himself and of the leading bishops of the East who shaped doctrinal discussion, and in subsequent decades the East, rather than Rome and the West, was the source of most of the new and significant theological ideas which were to emerge. Not until the Council of Chalcedon in 451 did a Roman bishop – Pope Leo the Great (440–461), by means of his *Letter* or *Tome* about the doctrine of the incarnation – make a significant contribution to the definition of doctrine, and even then it proved controversial and was not accepted without thorough debate and testing with reference to the views traditional among Eastern bishops.

In its sixth canon or ruling, concerning the powers of metropolitan bishops (i.e. the leading bishops of particular provinces) over the other churches of their provinces, the Council of Nicaea failed to give any special authority to Rome beyond what was enjoyed by Alexandria, Antioch, and the other metropolitan churches. This canon alone is sufficient to show that nothing could be further from the truth than to suggest that the Council of Nicaea was part of a papal scheme, contrived jointly with Constantine, for taking control of the whole church or imposing its particular theological agenda. The decision of the Council to define the Son of God as 'of one substance' with the Father was part of a widespread debate which was already of long standing, and did not require the intervention of the Pope to take the course it did. Nor, of course, is there any substance to the later legends that Constantine was baptized by Pope Silvester (and thus under his influence) or that he committed custody of the Western Roman empire to the Pope (the 'Donation of Constantine', which is a much later forgery).

Only towards the end of the fourth century do we find a clear recognition in the church as a whole that the Roman bishop enjoyed a primacy over the other leading bishops; this view is, however, taken for granted in the third canon of the Council of Constantinople of 381, which elevated Constantinople, the new imperial capital, to second place in the hierarchy of honour, 'because it is the new Rome'. But even then, it was to require nearly a century of further change – the decisions of church councils, imperial rulings, and papal initiatives – before this primacy on honour was to achieve, for the Western church, the reality of power. (In the East, as is well known, acceptance of papal authority was never as complete and continued to be contested.) By this time the size, status, wealth, and structure of the church had changed beyond all recognition compared with the pre-Constantinian period, and the power of the Papacy in the fifth century contrasts sharply with its much more modest role in the earlier period which it has been the main purpose of this chapter to explore.

To conclude then: theories that attribute to the Papacy a directive and sometimes sinister role in the early history of the church show little regard for the realities of the pre-Constantinian period, and can be accused of imposing on the early church an anachronistic picture, drawn from later centuries, of papal powers which the early Popes did not and indeed could not have wielded, given the undeveloped state of church organization. The Papacy grew into an institution more recognizable to us alongside the more general development of church government rather than as its controlling agent, and the shape of Christian doctrine was not the result of the imposition of a papal agenda. Until long after the time of Constantine, in fact, the Papacy was still only one among many factors shaping Christian history; the achievement of the position of dominance referred to at the beginning of this essay would be another story.

Further Reading

To understand the history of the early church, there is no substitute for reading early Christian writings. Most of the evidence discussed in this chapter is contained either in Eusebius's *Ecclesiastical History*, for which see G. A. Williamson and A. Louth, *Eusebius: the History of the Church* (Penguin; second edition, 1989), or in anthologies of early Christian documents, of which the best is probably still J. Stevenson and W. H. C. Frend, *A New Eusebius: Documents Illustrating the History of the Church to AD 337* (SPCK; new edition, 1987).

Much fuller accounts of the early history of the Papacy than this chapter will be found in any general history of the early church, e.g. the recent Ivor J. Davidson, *The Birth of the Church: From Jesus to Constantine, AD 30–312* and *A Public Faith: From Constantine to the Medieval World, AD 312–600* (The Monarch History of the Church, 1–2; Monarch Books, 2005). An accessible book which deals with the earliest period of the Roman church is James S. Jeffers, *Conflict at Rome: Social Order and Hierarchy in Early Christianity* (Fortress Press, 1991).

Chapter 4
What Is the Apocryphal New Testament?

Stuart Hall

The early Christian churches generated a great explosion of literature. The books they produced included the well-known books of the canonical New Testament. These are called 'canonical', because they have been 'ruled' to be those which should be read publicly in church and given special authority within the 'canon' (Greek *canon* = 'rule'). Most of the rest of their literature is lost. It was written on perishable material, and apart from being deliberately destroyed in persecution by Pagan, Muslim or Christian officials, copies all naturally perished as centuries passed. Only if someone took an interest would efforts be made to copy a text before the old copies perished, and later writers had other things to do. Our age is different: we busy ourselves piecing together the past from the scraps which history has left. A good deal remains. Often documents are found in remote corners of ancient Christianity, and have to be translated from languages like Syriac, Ethiopic or Coptic. Sometimes a book is preserved in various languages and versions. Modern researchers try to reconstruct an 'original', and to account for the various versions or fragments still surviving. Students of the New Testament books and of the older Hebrew and Greek bibles of ancient Israel have to do the same; though their usual problem is not that they have too little material to go on, but often far too much.

We now have some good and useful collections of material. Christian scholars often call the literature 'Apocrypha and Pseudepigrapha of the Old Testament' and 'Apocryphal New Testament'. These are not satisfactory terms, but conventional, and we shall use them here. The 'Apocrypha' of the Old Testament, books like *The Wisdom of Solomon* and two books of *Maccabees* are for many Christians (Roman Catholic, Eastern Orthodox and Anglican) part of the Bible. Protestants generally do not include them in the 'Canon'. Other ancient texts, mostly of Jewish origin, are called 'Pseudepigrapha', roughly meaning 'fictitious additional texts', and the books of *Enoch* and *Jubilees* fall into this class. 'Apocrypha' means literally 'hidden' or 'secret' things. It is not an ideal term for books which are openly available, and make no pretence to containing secrets. There are a few books which do make such claims, like the *Apocryphon of John*, which we shall discuss in the next chapter.

In addition to the Apocryphal books of the Old Testament, the word 'Apocrypha' is often applied to a large number of documents which in form resemble the books of the canonical New Testament, but are not included in the Canon. There are gospels which recount parts of Jesus' life and career, such as his birth, teaching or passion; there are books of acts of apostles, describing their missionary work or martyr-deaths; there are letters attributed to apostles or other ancient saints; and there are apocalypses or 'revelations' to apostles or ancient prophets, – a category of which the last book of the New Testament, John's *Revelation*, is a good example. There are apocryphal revelations to Peter, Paul and others.

Many 'Apocryphal New Testament' texts have been known for a long time. The number grows however. Sudden discoveries are sometimes made, the largest and most famous being in the thirteen Nag Hammadi Codices, which we discuss in the next chapter. This discovery adds a number of early documents which take the form, or have the titles, of 'gospel', 'epistle', 'acts' or 'apocalypse'. Some of these are now included in collections of Apocrypha. This has happened to the *Gospel of Philip* and the *Gospel of Thomas*. Apart from Nag Hammadi, papyrus fragments of this kind of literature turn up from time to time, some from known texts, some not otherwise known.

If difficult, the study of these works is also rewarding. It teaches us a great deal about how early Christians thought and wrote. The way they made up stories, or developed existing ones, may help us understand how the canonical books of the New Testament were themselves composed. The thoughts they set out to present are often alternatives to the estab-lished orthodox tradition, and this leads us to hope that they will throw light on the turbulent and varied religious movements which flowed from the life and passion of Jesus. It might even lead us to information about the traditions and stories circulating in the period before the books of the New Testament were written. Spectacular suggestions are sometimes made about 'the real Jesus', calling apocryphal texts in evidence. This is a very hazardous procedure. Before citing such texts, one has to ascertain whether they are based on the canonical texts, as nearly all of them certainly are, or whether they contain real vestiges of alternative ancient traditions, and finally whether such traditions are likely to be true.

One of the earliest and most popular 'Gospels' is the *Protevangelium of James* (Elliott 48–67; Hennecke 1. 421–438). 'Protevangelium' (Greek *Protevangelion*) means 'Pre-Gospel', referring to the fact that it is about Mary the Virgin, how she was born, reared and married, including the birth of Jesus. Parts have survived in over a hundred Greek manuscripts, some as early as the third century, as well as in various oriental languages. The *Protevangelium* was known to Clement of Alexandria (*c.*161–215) and Origen (*c.*185–251). It was probably written in the late second century. There is no Latin copy, presumably because it was condemned in the *Gelasian Decree*, a sixth-century list which was very influential, being attributed to various Popes (see Elliott 23–24; Hennecke 1. 38–40). The reason for rejecting the *Protevangelium* was that it makes Joseph of Nazareth the father of the brothers of Jesus; after St Jerome (died 420), Joseph was in the West regarded as always celibate and the 'brothers' as cousins. Parts of the story are retold in a number of Latin fictions.

In the *Protevangelium* Mary is herself conceived in answer to prayer by her childless parents Joachim and Anna, and dedicated to God at the age of three to serve in the Temple. The priests decide to give her in nominal marriage to an elderly widower, and by a miraculous sign Joseph is chosen for this role. He is to be in effect her guardian rather than her husband. At sixteen, while Mary is employed weaving a veil for the Temple, her life is interrupted by the angel who announces her coming pregnancy, an account expanding on Luke 1.26–38. She finishes her weaving and visits Elizabeth, again enlarging Luke. Joseph's reaction is based on Matthew 1.18–25, filled out with accounts of accusations and arguments about the legitimacy of the pregnancy. Joseph takes Mary on a donkey to Bethlehem for the census, but stops short because of the imminent birth. So Jesus is born in a wayside cave. The birth is miraculous, and Mary remains a virgin even while giving birth. This is an early, though not the earliest, statement of the Virgin Birth of Jesus (the canonical Gospels have only a virginal *conception* of Jesus, but his birth is apparently natural). Mary hears that Herod is trying to kill the child, so she wraps him in swaddling clothes and hides him in the manger. This is a good example of the way apocryphal writers weave together elements from different texts to make a new one; here the threat from Herod (Matthew 2.16) is combined with the manger (Luke 2.7).

The *Protevangelium* was never rejected in large parts of the Church, and its influence remains. Wherever there is a cult of Mary as 'ever-Virgin', wherever her own miraculous conception and birth are celebrated, or her mother Anna and father Joachim are portrayed in art, wherever Jesus is pictured born in a cave, wherever the legend is told of universal stillness at the moment of Christ's birth, and even where the ox stalled in the stable is accompanied in cribs and on Christmas cards by the ass which carried Mary there, the *Protevangelium* has left its mark. It begins the process towards the doctrine, held by Roman Catholics, of Mary's own Immaculate Conception.

Stories also arose in the ancient church to fill the gap in information between the earliest infancy of Jesus, his presentation in the Temple when forty days old (Luke 2.22–38) and his Passover visit when he was twelve (Luke 2.41–51). The best known collection is called *The Gospel of Thomas* (Elliott 68–83; Hennecke I. 439–443), or, since the discovery of the quite different *Gospel of Thomas* from Nag Hammadi, better called *The Infancy Gospel of Thomas*. A version was known to Origen, so it goes back to the early third century. It contains fictitious tales, mostly pretty silly, which show off the child's miraculous powers and knowledge. Many scholars, ancient and modern, believe that it has 'gnostic' features, in that the Saviour has these powers even in infancy. This 'gospel' survives in various versions and languages. The name of Thomas, who was highly revered by Christians in parts of Syria and India, and some features of the text, suggest that it was particularly popular in Syriac-speaking churches.

The earliest apocryphal account of the passion is the *Gospel of Peter*, preserved in only one incomplete copy (Elliott 150–158; Hennecke I. 216–227). The fragment starts at the point in the trial of Jesus where Pilate washes his hands; it recounts the mocking, crucifixion and burial of Jesus, reading mostly like an abbreviated pastiche of the four canonical texts, with occasional variations. Jesus, for instance, is silent 'as if he felt no pain' (*Gospel of Peter* 4.10), when he is crucified. In the canonical texts it is during interrogation that this silence occurs (Mark 14.61; 15.4,5 and parallels; John 19.9). This silence itself reflects a typological use of Isaiah 53.7, where God's servant is silent like a lamb led to slaughter, and *Peter* ties it closely to the crucifixion itself. The superscription on the cross says, 'This is the King of Israel'. The canonical accounts, though all differing from each other, all have 'the King of the Jews'. The change reflects *Peter*'s sense of alienation from the Jews, who in his account physically manage the crucifixion. The resurrection of Jesus takes place in full view of the watching guard and Jewish elders, with miraculous elaborations. A voice from heaven refers to Christ's having preached to the dead in the time between his dying and rising, which indicates that the text is later than the canonical gospels. The surviving copy breaks off after the women see an angelic youth in Christ's tomb, and as Simon Peter (who calls himself 'I, Simon Peter') has gone to his home and sets out fishing. He is accompanied by Andrew and Levi (and perhaps others). An appearance of the risen Lord at the lakeside presumably followed, as in John 21.

We cannot tell how much went before, or whether *The Gospel of Peter* was simply a narrative of the passion and resurrection. It is fairly certain however that this fragment, which has no title, is part of the *Gospel of Peter* mentioned by Origen and by Eusebius (Eusebius, *Ecclesiastical history*, 6.12 and 3.3.1–2). Eusebius reports that Serapion, Bishop of Antioch about 180–200, told the church in the Syrian town of Rhossus that he was withdrawing his permission to read this gospel, because his attention had been drawn to heretical features. Eusebius accepts the condemnation, and includes this gospel among writings not received as Catholic Scriptures. This rejection accounts for the absence of surviving copies. The likeliest place for finding heresy in the surviving text is the Lord's cry from the cross, 'My power, power, you have forsaken me' (5.18), a version of the cry recorded in Matthew 27.46 and Mark 15.34, 'My God, my God, why have you forsaken me?' Some sects held that divine power entered the man Jesus at his baptism, and left him before he suffered on the cross. Several features unique to *The Gospel of Peter* appear in *Peri Pascha*, an Easter homily or liturgy composed by Melito of Sardis between 160 and 180 (*Peri Pascha* 72–99). Notably Melito has Christ's trial and execution led and performed by King Herod and the Jews, as in this *Gospel*. This develops a minor role played by Herod in one canonical Gospel, Luke 23.6–12, and a general tendency of early Christians to blame the Jews rather than Pontius Pilate for Jesus' execution.

The exculpation of Pilate is already developing in the canonical gospels, but progresses as Pilate is more emphatically cleared of responsibility, and even sanctified for trying to save Jesus from death. Various *Acts of Pilate* (Elliott 164–225; Hennecke 1 501–536) are mentioned as early as the second century, and the same title is used for an anti-Christian account of the trial of Jesus published by one of the last persecuting regimes in 311–312. The surviving *Acts of Pilate*, in various versions and languages, is probably later still, but might use earlier sources. It purports to be written, originally in Hebrew, by Nicodemus (a biblical figure: John 3.1–15; 7.50–52; 19.39–42), and is sometimes called *The Gospel of Nicodemus*. It is followed by an account of Christ's descent into Hades, and the release of all the saints of old, including Adam. This part is aimed to fill out the mysterious statements in 1 Peter 3.18–19 and 4.6, but also reflects controversy with some early groups who denied the salvation of Adam, as between Irenaeus and Tatian. There are supplementary documents, like the correspondence between Pilate and the Roman emperors Tiberius and Claudius. All are pious fictions.

Gospel literature includes some early Hebrew or Aramaic/Syriac texts used by groups associated with Judaeo-Christianity. This is just the sort of material most likely to give us insights into Christian origins different from those in the main tradition and the canonical documents. The New Testament itself contains many indications that the churches in Jerusalem and Judaea differed from those dominated by the tradition of St Paul. Paul's letter to the Galatians, for instance, shows him strenuously asserting his independence from the church of Jerusalem, led by Cephas (= Simon Peter) and James, which consisted predominantly of converts from Judaism. This James is referred to as 'the Lord's brother'. According to Galatians, James and his associates have serious problems about whether Gentile believers in Christ should be circumcised, and whether circumcised believers were permitted to eat with the uncircumcised, and Peter partly shared these reservations. A serious quarrel with Paul is reported in Galatians 2, and in a number of places in *Acts* (especially Chapter 15) it is clear that the author presents such quarrels as amicably settled, when in fact they probably went very deep. There was apparently a Judaean church whose members believed in keeping the laws about the Sabbath, circumcision and kosher food, which many Gentile converts, led by Paul, did not. If we could find traditions about Jesus and the first churches deriving from these communities, we might find real historical supplements to what the New Testament tells us. The New Testament itself contains some documents which perhaps come from Palestinian and Jewish Christianity, for instance the letters of James and Jude, and some of the traditions behind the birth and infancy stories in Luke. In one or two matters the nature of this non-Pauline Christianity can be illuminated also by information from the Dead Sea Scrolls. These were produced by the intense charismatic and monastic sects which lived by the Dead Sea in the time of Jesus, with whom John the Baptist was probably associated (see Chapter 6).

Unfortunately we know the gospel or gospels used by such Jewish or Judaizing believers only through references and fragments in orthodox writers of the next three centuries, like Clement of Alexandria, Origen, Eusebius, Didymus the Blind and especially Jerome and Epiphanius. There are also some notes in the manuscripts of Matthew with textual readings from 'The Jewish'; these are probably quoted from a lost commentary on Matthew. These sources confuse us by using different titles for the books concerned, though most of them speak as if there were one gospel 'of the Hebrews' or 'according to the Hebrews'. Sometimes these later writers borrow quotations from each other, rather than directly copying from the gospel itself. Sorting such material out is consequently very difficult, and the results are uncertain. The most favoured solution identifies three such documents:

1. *The Gospel according to the Hebrews.* This appears to have been written in Greek early in the second century. All the quotations seem to be fictitious developments based on New Testament material. One of the seven fragments tells how Christ rose from the dead and appeared to James the Just, an episode apparently based upon 1 Corinthians 15.7 and the Emmaus Road episode of Luke 24.13–31 (Elliott Fragment 3; Hennecke Fragment 7).

2. *The Gospel of the Ebionites.* This name is used by modern scholars for a work which Epiphanius in the late fourth century thought belonged to the sect called 'Ebionites'. It is usually assumed that this group was a continuation of the primitive Jerusalem church, who might have called themselves *ebionim*, meaning 'Poor' in Hebrew; compare St Paul's collections in aid of 'the poor' in Jerusalem (Galatians 2.10 and elsewhere). For all we know, however, the sect may be a later attempt to revive the communal life of the church as described in Acts 2–4. This gospel develops different canonical stories and included additions to familiar stories. So when Jesus was baptized, a great light shone, and the story manages to include three versions of the divine words: 'You are my son, and in you am I well pleased,' from Mark 1.11, 'This day have I begotten you,' from some manuscripts of Luke 3.22, and 'This is my beloved son, in whom I am well pleased' of Matthew 3.17 (Elliott Fragment 3; Hennecke Fragment 7).

3. *The Gospel of the Nazaraeans.* A rather small group who lived near Beroea in Syria were known as Nazarenes or Nazaraeans. They had what Jerome and other church writers thought was a version of the original Hebrew Gospel of Matthew. It is now thought to have existed rather in Aramaic or Syriac than Hebrew, and to be based upon our Greek Matthew rather than its original. Thus the episode of the man

in the synagogue with a withered hand (Matthew 12.9–14 and parallels) is enlarged, so that he appeals to Jesus, saying he is a mason, unable to work because of his disability (Elliott fragment 9; Hennecke fragment 10). Yet again, we are faced with changes which follow on the canonical Gospels, and not convincing primitive alternatives.

Those who look for a Christology, an interpretation of the person of Jesus Christ, which treats him as a man and not as God, will be disappointed by these apocryphal gospels. The writers who record most of the fragments, Epiphanius and Jerome, though anxious to trash the 'Hebrew Gospel', produce no such statements. The *Gospel of the Nazaraeans* is said to be generally like Matthew, but lacks the birth stories, starting, as Mark does, with the baptism of Jesus. That could indicate that the virginal conception is rejected, a position the Ebionites may have held. But it could equally signify rejection of his genuine physical humanity, as is the case in Marcion's gospel, as we shall see in the next chapter; in that case, it is his divinity, not his humanity, that is being exaggerated. Emphasis is also laid on the 'whole fountain of the Holy Spirit' descending on Jesus at his baptism, and the words, 'This day I have begotten you' (*Gospel of the Ebionites* 5 in Elliott = 3 in Hennecke). To some that suggests an 'adoptionist' Christology, in which Christ is not the Son of God before his human birth, but a man adopted into that status. Yet both these ideas, the fulness of the Spirit, and the idea that Christ was a man who was promoted to the status of God, are present in the canonical texts (John 1.32–34; Acts 2.36). Jesus speaks of the Holy Spirit as his mother (*Gospel according to the Hebrews* 2). So it is difficult to get a 'low' or humanist Christology out of this material.

Other less important gospels and gospel-fragments exist. We cannot discuss them all. It is time to turn to some of the apocryphal *Acts* of Apostles. Churches early on started celebrating saints. This applied to martyrs in particular. But the Apostles, the first heirs of Jesus' authority in the Church, were especially remembered. The canonical books include some stories about them, and *The Acts of the Apostles* in particular has a great deal to say about Paul, with others like Peter, James of Jerusalem, and the deacons Stephen and Philip also figuring. Particular churches regarded particular saints as their own. A church needed a story to read when the saint was celebrated, usually on the anniversary of his purported martyrdom. Such 'Acts' originate in the second or third centuries, and go on developing in various times and places down the ages. Though not so obviously unorthodox as to be everywhere condemned in the wider church, they sometimes reflect attitudes and spirituality usually associated with 'gnosticism'. They also tend to be 'encratite', which means they expect a man or woman to give up marriage and sexual relations on receiving baptism. All are full of dramatic miracles, the raising of dead individuals being often used to persuade observers to believe the Gospel. None are copied complete in our sources, so editors have to put the broken bits together, and sort out the older from the newer bits.

The chief surviving *Acts* are those of Andrew, John, Paul, Peter and Thomas. Andrew travels in Greece (in some traditions, in Scythia, i.e. southern Russia), where he gets into trouble and is ultimately executed for converting the proconsul's wife to sexual abstinence. This was probably only the end-part, or *passio*, of a much longer book, since a Latin abridgement survives (by Gregory of Tours, sixth century), giving a long set of miracle stories.

The *Acts of John* is set in Asia Minor, and is full of resurrections and conversions to the celibate life. This work contains some interesting early sermons and liturgical texts, remarkable for the naïf way in which Christ is acknowledged as God and worshipped in a sacred dance. The cross is a universal symbol, and there is an attempt to resolve the problem of how the Logos or Word of God can be understood as having suffered: the universal divine being spoke to John on the Mount of Olives even while the people watched him being crucified below. The Lord's body is of varying physical nature even before his passion, being not always solid.

The *Acts of Paul* is not completely preserved. In it, among much other entertaining narrative, are three parts especially popular with later Christians: (1) *The Acts of Paul and Thecla*, a version of which was certainly known before 200, (2) an exchange of letters with the Corinthian church ('3 Corinthians'), and (3) Paul's trial and execution by the emperor Nero.

(1) Thecla has a charming feminist story. Saved from the threat of matrimony by Paul's preaching of virginity, she is protected by a rich woman and a lioness during various persecutions instigated by her disappointed fiancé, baptizes herself in a pool in the arena, and ends up as an evangelist, miracle-worker and teacher. (2) Paul's additional letter to the Corinthians is provoked by a letter from them, outlining the heretical teachings which are troubling them about the authority of the Old Testament, whether God the creator is almighty, the resurrection of the body, the reality of Christ's birth in the flesh, and whether the world

was made by angels. All these themes were heard among those the second-century church rejected as 'gnostic' heretics, and are here naturally rejected by Paul. (3) As to Paul's martyrdom, his beheading follows on the conversion of close guards and associates of the emperor Nero and various direct interviews between him and Paul. Like the other narratives, it reflects information gathered from various New Testament books and is imaginatively filled out.

The surviving *Acts of Peter* consist chiefly of an account of Peter's coming to Rome after Paul left for Spain on a missionary journey. The Roman church was threatened by the teaching of Simon Magus ('the Magician'; see Acts 8.9–24). Simon was reckoned the founding father of all the heresies by the orthodox from the second century onwards. Peter, arrives in Rome, reconverts many of those whom Simon had drawn away from the true faith by a series of miracles, which include a talking dog and raising the dead to life. In a final competition of miracles, Simon flies up in the air above Rome, but falls and is seriously injured as a result of Peter's prayers. As Peter leaves Rome in the face of persecution, Christ meets him and sends him back to die, which he does, crucified head downwards. In the second chapter Paul offers the eucharistic sacrifice with bread and water, an interesting example of the abstinence from wine common among encratite Marcionite and other Christians. There are less clear examples of the same practice in *Acts of John* 85 and *Acts of Thomas* 87. These imaginary sacramental scenes give precious information about how worship was practised in the circles which created and used these *Acts*.

Peter and his rival Simon the Magician also star in the extensive Pseudo-Clementine literature, a collection chiefly from the early third century, but including some early Jewish-Christian elements, and worked over in later times in various theological interests. While important information may be buried under these fanciful and intriguing documents, the task of sorting out the details is very controversial, and we leave it undiscussed (see Hennecke II. 483–541).

The last of the great ancient biographies is the *Acts of Thomas*. In this, 'Judas Thomas, also called Didymus' (see Chapter 2), is allotted by the Apostles the mission to India, a territory which had considerable connexions with both Egypt and Syria. As was mentioned in Chapter 2, his Aramaic name 'Thomas', like the Greek 'Didymus', means 'twin', and Judas is taken to be the twin brother of Jesus himself. He is a familiar figure as the chief apostle to Syrian Christians centring on Edessa, and in

India. In the story of the conversion of the royal family Jesus sometimes intervenes, being identical in appearance with Thomas. Thomas arrives in time to persuade the king's only daughter to forsake her impending marriage and be baptized. Various persecutions, debates and miracles follow, leading to the king's conversion. Amid this historical fantasy we find important things of interest to modern scholars. Baptisms take place, in which anointing with oil precedes baptism, or even seems to displace it (*Acts of Thomas* 121, 132, 157). The prayers at baptism and eucharist are a valuable liturgical record reflecting the time and place of their composition. Some versions of the *Acts* include what was originally an independent poem, 'The hymn of the pearl' (*Acts of Thomas* 108–113). This hymn celebrates the king's son, who leaves his precious jewelled robe behind in the east to go to Egypt and recover a precious pearl, guarded by an evil dragon. Falling asleep, he is roused by a message from home, fulfils his mission, returns home, recovers his robe, and is presented to his father. This has been regarded as a (possibly pre-Christian) 'gnostic' myth. It is however full of biblical images and typology (like the pearl of Matthew 13.45–46, and the son lost and found in Luke 15.11–32), and it probably belongs to early Syrian Christianity.

Early Christian fictions included letters or 'Epistles'. Some letters in the New Testament were not written by their ostensible authors, but were probably compiled by disciples who wrote, as they saw it, with the authority of the named apostle. Some of the later fictions are mild and unimportant, like the letter of Paul to the Laodiceans. It is a short compilation of phrases from other letters of Paul, filling the gap indicated by Colossians 4.16. A popular fiction was the series of Latin letters between Paul and Seneca, a highly regarded Stoic philosopher who, like Paul, was a victim of one of Nero's purges. It naturally argues the truth of Christianity and the evil of persecution. There is a long Epistle attributed to Paul's associate Titus, written in bad Latin. Its purpose is to promote celibate and virginal life, and it is of interest for the use it makes of the various apocryphal *Acts* of apostles, as well as of orthodox writers like Cyprian and Jerome. It probably originated in the Spanish charismatic and monastic Priscillianist movement in the fifth century. The so-called *Epistula Apostolorum* or 'Letter of the Apostles' is an early document, which deals with some second-century problems of ethical conduct and church order, early heresies, and the end of the world. But it is an account of conversations between the apostles and Jesus after his resurrection, and should rather be classed with various documents which claim apostolic authority for religious practice, whether new or already established (*Didache* or *The Teaching of the Apostles* is the earliest of these). There are some 'Epistles' also in the Nag Hammadi collection.

The final class of New Testament Apocrypha is that of Apocalypses, 'Revelations'. As with letters, a number of these appear in the Nag Hammadi set, and we shall consider some in the next chapter.

Among other apocalypses, the most important are *The Apocalypse of Peter* and *The Apocalypse of Paul*.

The *Apocalypse of Peter* was known and used as scripture by a number of early church writers, such as Theophilus of Antioch, Clement of Alexandria and Methodius, and it must have been written before the middle of the second century. Later it was regarded as dubious, and it was lost. A late copy of the whole in Ethiopic, and a rediscovered Greek revision of part of it, enable us to see what it said. It has similarities to the *Gospel of Peter*, including 'I, Peter' as the spokesman. Jesus meets the apostles on the Mount of Olives (implicitly, after the resurrection, as with many apocryphal accounts), and requests guidance about the meaning of the fig-tree parables. The language and discussion are all based closely on canonical gospel material. Peter is given descriptions and visions of the judgment of the last days, of the torments of the damned in the river of fire, and the beauties of paradise. The detail of all this is the first example of many Christian accounts of the torments of the damned in hell, which were thought to be useful for promoting good behaviour. The transfiguration of Jesus (Mark 9.2–8 and parallels, and 2 Peter 1.16–18) surprisingly turns up, apparently in connexion with the blessings of the elect. The reason for the rejection and suppression of this once popular apocalypse may be that it appears to allow the ultimate salvation of some or all of the damned, in response to the prayers of the righteous. Such a hope was reckoned destructive of public morals.

The *Apocalypse of Paul* is a later composition, perhaps originally of the third century. It survives in many editions and versions. It takes up the clue of Paul's ascent to the third heaven and paradise, guardedly described by him in 2 Corinthians 12.1–5. It contains elaborate descriptions of souls being judged by God, and the punishment of the damned and the bliss of the righteous. Its Latin version, puporting to have been discovered in Paul's home in Tarsus in AD 388, was very influential in the medieval West.

In conclusion, we might say that we have been able to survey the more important of the early Christian apocrypha. The fertile imagination of those ancient believers threw up plenty of literature. Some of this we shall discuss in the next chapter.

We have left out a lot. Apart from omitting less important works, we have excluded the so-called 'Apostolic Fathers', 'orthodox' works not claiming to be apostolic. These include various letters, and one enormous prophetic revelation, *The Shepherd* by Hermas of Rome. But from what we have seen it is apparent that apocryphal and gnostic writers usually take texts from the canonical New Testament as the norm and basis. Delicate analysis may uncover independent sayings and acts of Jesus in *The Gospel of Thomas* and the Jewish-Christian fragments, but these are at best uncertain and do not undermine what the canonical books tell us. They do however show us how early believers were prepared to build on, edit, correct, and interpret the scriptures they believed in, both the Old Testament and the New. That lets us see better how the canonical books themselves were composed, and how what they say should be understood in relation to the historical facts they describe or represent. The Apocrypha attest a developing, varied and lively faith, based firmly in the idea that in the risen Jesus God had spoken finally, directly and uniquely to humanity.

Perhaps a further word is needed about story-telling. Before the time of Christ the great philosopher Plato puritanically condemned the stories of poets, which he thought demeaned God. Yet when it came to fundamental questions about the origin of the world and the good and evil in it, he gave up rational explanation and told stories or 'myths': the one about the Craftsman or Demiurge would profoundly affect not only Valentinian theology, but the kind of thinking about Jesus which we find in the Nicene Creed. The Christian Bible is in any case full of stories. From them we are expected to learn the ways of God with mankind, and the right and wrong ways for men to approach God. After the Bible was formed, and even while it was being written, people have gone on telling and retelling the stories to give them more impact, to make them relevant to their own time, to clear up difficulties. Medieval miracle plays did it. Modern films, plays and books about Jesus, and about the Bible, regularly do it; though it seemed a new thing in the middle of the twentieth century when Dorothy Sayers wrote *The Man Born to be King* for sound radio. At a lowly level, every school Nativity Play is a new apocryphal book. It puts together things you read in different parts of the Bible. Then it simplifies the language and adds bits of dialogue. Songs and carols are put in, or perhaps dance. New characters are added too: the inn-keeper and wife may be named, and Father Christmas may pay a visit, complete with reindeer (even Mickey Mouse). In the same tradition, people try to improve the whole historical tradition of Christian faith. *The Holy Blood and the Holy Grail* is a splendid piece of apocryphal story-writing, using the facts and records of the Christian past to rewrite its history. *The Da Vinci Code* is pure fiction, but good fun. It would be very unwise for those who love God in Jesus Christ to object to this. Story-telling is at the heart of their faith. Condemning religious stories and sentencing story-tellers to death with a *fatwa* cannot be right: God's honour does not need us to defend it, and killing story-tellers is far more blasphemous than telling risky religious tales. Without stories, the Christian faith would die; we cannot do without them. We just have to understand how the process works, and use them well.

Further Reading

There are two basic modern collections: J. K. Elliott, *The Apocryphal New Testament. A Collection of Apocryphal Christian Texts in an English translation* (Clarendon Press, 1993; cited as 'Elliott'), and E. Hennecke and W. Schneemelcher, *New Testament Apocrypha* (English translation ed. by R. McL. Wilson, 2 vols, rev. ed. James Clark, 1991; cited as Hennecke; the old 1963/1965 edition is still usable). There are useful studies in *The Cambridge History of Christianity I: Origins to Constantine*, ed. Margaret M. Mitchell and Frances M. Young (Cambridge University Press, 2006). For the history of the Canon see Hennecke I 9–75; H. Y. Gamble, *The New Testament Canon: Its Making and Meaning* (Fortress Press, 1985) and Bruce M. Metzger, *The Canon of the New Testament: Its Origin, Development, and Significance* (Clarendon Press,1987). On Judaeo-Christianity see P. Vielhauer and G. Strecker in Hennecke I 134–178; more briefly Elliott 3–16, and pp.213–364 of *A Companion to Second-Century Christian 'Heretics'*, ed. Antti Marjanen and Petri Luomanen (Brill, 2005; *Supplements to Vigiliae Christianae* 76).

Chapter 5

What Was Gnosticism?

Stuart Hall

'Gnosticism' is important for understanding the early Church and its
books, but is a slippery concept. The different ways the word is used
mean that even the best scholars must be read with caution when the
words 'gnostic', 'gnosticism' or 'gnosis' appear. *Gnosis* is Greek for
'knowledge', and a *gnostikos* means one who claims or practises knowledge at a high level. Gnosis was not quite the same as factual or scientific
knowledge. Ancient thinkers who followed Plato regarded it as a higher
way of knowing things, superior to the 'opinion' or 'belief' involved in
observed facts. One important scholar, handling the writings usually
labelled 'gnostic', translates it as 'acquaintance', which is itself perhaps
not solemn or serious enough (see Bentley Layton).

Early believers in Christ valued knowledge, especially knowing
God and being known by him (see John 17.3; 1 John 4.7–8), even if
knowledge had its limitations (1 Corinthians 8.1–3, 13.12). For some
writers in the orthodox tradition, knowledge was the goal of sacred
study, the height to which God would lift the devout ascetic and student.
Clement of Alexandria (*c.*161–215), Origen (*c.*185–251), and Evagrius
Ponticus (a great monastic writer, 355–399), all regarded becoming
a *gnostikos* as the highest spiritual goal. But already before Clement
'gnosis falsely so called' (1 Timothy 6.20) and its 'gnostic' adherents
were a major object of attack, especially by Irenaeus about AD 180.

There are three chief ways of understanding gnosis and gnosticism.
First there is the classic Christian way, in which most ancient writers
followed Irenaeus. It is like a great ancient 'school' of philosophy (such
as Platonism); it had a continuing tradition with various teachers. So
Irenaeus lumped together as 'gnostics' a number of schools of thought,
with names like 'Naassenes' or founding fathers like Valentinus,
Basilides, – or Irenaeus' local opponent Markos. This idea of the gnostic
'heresy' as a many-headed version or perversion of Christianity has
prevailed down the centuries, and continued into modern times. Not
only did traditional Christian thinkers accept it, but so did outstanding
modern critics, like Adolf Harnack in the late nineteenth century, who

saw gnosticism as a forward-looking intellectual movement: gnosticism was part of second-century Church history.

The second understanding of gnosticism picks out some ideas and features common to a number of these groups, and claims they came from a pre-Christian religion, which is called 'Gnosis'. Much confusion was caused when English-language scholars translated this as 'gnosticism'. This religion was alleged to have originated in Iran. That was certainly true of the religion of Mani (founded AD 240), whose views were based on the dualism of light and darkness in ancient Persian Zoroastrianism: the world was not made by one God, but was the battlefield between two divine principles, good/light and evil/darkness. Some form of dualism, where a realm of pure goodness and light is separate from and not responsible for this world and its evils, is found in various of the early Christian sects. But this religion was claimed to be pre-Christian, influencing much of the New Testament. It appears especially in the 'gnostic redeemer myth', the story of the figure sent from the realm of light to gather the fragments of his own original light, which were somehow imprisoned in darkness, and to restore them to the spiritual world where they belong. This idea of 'gnosis as a world-religion' was propagated by the so-called 'religious history school' in Germany. There it also became a prominent tool in the New Testament theology of Rudolf Bultmann and his followers. Gnosis was seen as a way of understanding both the New Testament and the whole human predicament in the twentieth century. This presentation as a world-religion has encouraged modern people to think that Gnosticism/Gnosis is a valid alternative religion for modern times, as can be seen by looking up the word on any of many websites (see also Hans Jonas). Later, under the impact of new discoveries, this idea of a pre-Christian gnostic religion has been generally dropped; but not before it had influenced the early interpretations of the new texts, which are explained below (p.64ff). It seriously affects the otherwise magnificent handbook of Kurt Rudolph.

The third view of gnosticism is that there was an original or 'classic' gnostic movement. Irenaeus and others like him are to blame for expanding the designation to embrace other sects and ideas, like those of Valentinus and Basilides, who are often still called 'gnostics'. This view has advantages, especially as the larger part of the new finds consists of books from this school. Its members may be called 'Sethian' or 'Sethian gnostic', because Seth, Adam's third son, is their hero and redeemer figure. These are regarded by many scholars, notably Bentley Layton, as the original gnostics. They clearly used Old Testament texts and ideas, but their use of the New Testament is less obvious.

Before looking at some detail, a word is needed about the immense vitality of early Christianity, before a general organization, creed, or even Bible had established itself. Church groups generally had some sacred texts. Originally these were parts of the Old Testament, usually in Greek. Gradually they accumulated apostolic letters, stories of Jesus and other documents, but chiefly they lived by the Spirit with festive initiations and meals. Later it was claimed that among the first apostolic churches there was unanimity in faith, organization and practice; but we now know that that was false. Many practices and beliefs later condemned as 'heresy' were for their adherents the first or only Gospel truth they knew. A 'heresy' (Greek *hairesis*) meant originally an 'option' or a 'party'. Early Christian writers like Irenaeus saw their own views as traditional, as the only truth handed on faithfully by Christ's apostles and their successors: heresies or parties were human inventions, created by adding to, subtracting from, or distorting that truth. Heresy was seen as having a life of its own, and one generation after another of heretics would follow and develop what others had said. Simon Magus of Acts 8.9–24 was regarded as the first heretic, and all later errors were traced back to him. This is one reason why Simon is the main opponent of St. Peter in apocryphal texts, as we shall see. It was useful to describe more recent schools and sects in terms of past heresies already condemned. So a picture emerged of heretical uniformity, of a kind of genetic similarity, between groups and teachers who in fact differed widely from each other.

This partly explains why the word 'gnostic' came to embrace not only the Sethians, but important thinkers like Valentinus, Basilides and Marcion, whose works are largely lost. The Manichees, and in later ages the Cathars, could all be lumped together as gnostics, and scholars have to piece together from the rude and disparaging accounts of their critics what second-century writers may have said. This lumping together is something we should avoid. That applies not only to using 'Gnostic' to cover a great variety of thinkers like Basilides and Valentinus. It is now seen as better to avoid the common practice of labelling other writers 'Valentinian', 'Basilidean' or 'Marcionite': Basilides' son Isidore should be read in his own right; the writings of Theodotus in the east and Ptolemy and Heracleon in the west are better not quoted as examples of 'Valentinianism'; and Marcion's 'successor' Apelles was not a pure

'Marcionite'. 'Heresy' and 'gnosticism' were no more united and
single than was the 'catholic' or universal Christianity which came
to prevail.

We have mentioned new finds. The most important are the thirteen
Nag Hammadi Codices, which were discovered high up the Nile in
Egypt in December 1945. A 'codex' means a book of pages in the shape
of a modern book, as distinct from the scroll or roll like those found
near the Dead Sea. The Nag Hammadi Codices contain about 47 texts
in Coptic (the Christian Egyptian language); some of them are copied
more than once. They are probably all translated from Greek. Some are
in good condition, others seriously damaged. All are still the subject of
laborious work and analysis. The texts were copied down about AD 350,
but had often been written much earlier, in the first or second century.
Most have however been altered by editing and translation. The codices
were found in an area where thousands of Christian monks and nuns
lived in settled communities in the fifth century. The books collected have
monastic features: sexual continence is highly regarded, wealth despised,
and occasionally the mainstream churches are criticized. So it is likely
the books belonged to such a community. They were buried in a big
sealed jar, perhaps when their owners were dispossessed or persecuted
by more orthodox groups. The reason they are such a treasure to us is
that, though they are later copies, the originals were written much earlier,
and they come from groups whose works are otherwise lost.

These and other finds have helped us understand how some of the
ancient Christians thought and prayed. We now look at a few examples.
The most important, perhaps, is *The Apocryphon* [= Secret Book] *of
John*. There are three copies of it among the Nag Hammadi books, and
another in a separate but obviously related treasure, 'The Berlin Codex'.
Two are of a shorter, two of a longer version. Substantial parts of the text
were known to Irenaeus in the second century.

The Apocryphon has a narrative beginning and end: Jesus appears
after the ascension to John the son of Zebedee, who is despondent at his
inability to answer a Pharisee's critical questions. This framework makes
it a Christian book. What lies between however, though clearly indebted
to the Old Testament, is not at all obviously Christian. It is an account of
what happened before the creation of the world as set out in Genesis, and
an interpretation of the stories of Adam and Eve and some subsequent
biblical history. The reader should be warned that to read the bare text is
to expose oneself to what looks like a farrago of nonsensical names and

ideas. (It is as well to read it in a version which has commentary and analysis, like B. Layton's.)

The 'Father of everything' ('Parent of the entirety'), or Great Invisible Spirit, though strictly single, has various names. This Spirit's 'Thought' takes shape as a figure called Barbelo or Christ, who obtains qualities belonging to the Spirit: prior knowledge, incorruptibility, eternal life, and truth. Barbelo is appointed to generate other spiritual beings, which have the names either of spiritual qualities (like prudence, beauty) or else mysterious Semitic-sounding names. The chief are the four 'luminaries', who figure in almost every version of the 'Gnostic myth': Harmozel, Oroiael, Daueithe and Eleleth. With these are associated groups of other figures, including heavenly prototypes of Adam (Geradamas) and Seth his holy son, and of Eve (Wisdom). Thus is constituted a spiritual order. The beings in it are often called 'aeons' (or 'eons'), using the Greek word *aion*, which means an 'age', 'realm' or 'world'. Together, in some forms of the myth, the aeons are called the 'fulness' or 'entirety' (Greek *pleroma*). In *The Apocryphon*, as in most versions of the myth, this physical world, its god, its angels, its entirety, come about because the aeon Wisdom (Sophia) wants to produce an image of herself by herself without the consent of her partner or the great Spirit. Her offspring is Ialtabaoth (also spelled Ialdabaoth, Altabaoth), the 'First Ruler', an ambiguous but generally evil figure. He is the god of this world, and of the creation stories of Genesis. In other texts he can also be called Saklas or Satan. He creates a whole army of angelic or demonic figures, the Rulers (Archons), who help him make the world. The creation of Adam is explained in bizarre detail, including both a soul and a body. Ialtabaoth boasts that he alone is God, and has to be corrected. Wisdom tries to rectify the results of her folly, and does so by getting Ialtabaoth to breathe her spirit into the lifeless body of Adam. Seth, Adam's son, becomes the repository of the Mother's spirit, and his descendants, 'the immovable race', will grow in spiritual life and finally be restored to 'the repose of the aeons'. Others, deceived and misled, will remain under the Rulers. *The Apocryphon* ends with a poem of deliverance, which celebrates the coming of Christ, and resurrection bestowed on believers through 'five seals' – initiation rites which include some kind of baptism.

The broad pattern of the history or the two kinds of beings, the spiritual, populated with aeons emanating from the primal Spirit, and the lower, the work of the Rulers and their chief Ialtabaoth, is repeated in various other documents. The accounts of the spiritual beings vary in detail, though the broad outlines, especially the Christ or Barbelo, the first being originated from the Father, the four Luminaries, and the folly or error of Sophia producing the lower world, are constant. Similarly the varied retelling of the Old Testament stories, especially Genesis: God is the bad Ialtabaoth, and the immovable race, the spiritual people who inherited the knowledge Eve got from the tree (forbidden by Ialtabaoth), are the descendants of the spiritual Seth.

How does all this relate to Christianity? Plainly *The Apocryphon of John* was christianized by its frame-story. We have an even clearer example in the Nag Hammadi collection. We have two copies of *Eugnostos the Blessed*, a kind of epistle giving a philosophical version of the myth of what happened before time, and two copies of *The Sophia (Wisdom) of Jesus Christ*, where exactly the same teaching, and more, is given in a discussion between Jesus after his resurrection, and twelve disciples and seven women on a mountain in Galilee. Unquestionably the Sethian gnostic myth has been Christianized in the longer book. The question scholars have debated is whether the myth itself was pre-Christian or non-Christian.

The Sethian mythology certainly has Old Testament elements. This points to either Jewish or Christian influence. Not only are the 'upside-down' interpretation of the creation and other Genesis stories about this world obviously biblical, but also behind the complexities of the transcendent realm there often lie spiritualized interpretations of the Bible. Philo the Jewish philosopher, a contemporary of Jesus Christ, taught that the first chapter of Genesis described the making of the heavenly and spiritual order, not of this world, and that the second chapter recounted the making of the first physical human beings. In this he was followed by the most famous theologians in the early Church, like Origen and Augustine of Hippo. So it is no surprise to find in Sethianism not only an original Father superior to the fickle Ialtabaoth, who is the god of Old Testament history, but among the eternal aeons the proto-types of Seth and of Adam his father (called Adamas or Geradamas). Even the wayward Sophia is probably modelled on the biblical Eve: she strives for divinity and for knowledge, and causes catastrophe, but then becomes the instrument of salvation, just as the earthly Eve gives birth to Seth, the holy seed.

Before going further we must emphasize that the Sethian gnosticism we have concentrated on is only one of several movements usually called 'gnostic'. This is partly because most of the Nag Hammadi documents are of this kind, but also because in most modern studies the Sethian form is considered basic and prior to others. Here we can only give an outline of some of the others.

Probably the most important of these movements is associated with Valentinus, a theologian from Alexandria who went to Rome and worked there: early Christian sources place him in Rome about AD 140. The fragments of Valentinus' works are very few, and not enough to understand his system (see Layton 229–247). They do reflect serious thought on biblical passages: how the image of God functions in Adam, how you become pure in heart, how Jesus' digestive system worked. With Valentinus are associated two western figures of the later second century, Ptolemy and Heracleon. Ptolemy is known by a single writing, his *Letter to Flora* (Layton 206–219). It is a careful explanation of the complexities of the Pentateuch, the first five books of the Old Testament. Taking up some remarks of Jesus in the Gospels, Ptolemy distinguishes what comes from God, what comes from Moses, and what comes from the Elders. The god who created the law is imperfect, and has a higher, perfect God above him. The whole discussion, as with Valentinus, is conducted in terms of Christian scriptures. The same applies to Heracleon, who wrote the first commentary known to us on a New Testament book. His work on John's Gospel was used by Origen in his own commentary; it reflects a desire to find spiritual truths in apparently physical historical events. In Alexandria the 'Valentinian' Theodotus was a Christian thinker, whose writings were read, generally sympathetically, and annotated by Clement of Alexandria, an orthodox writer of about AD 200.

Irenaeus gives a fairly full account of the beliefs of the Valentinians. He knew a local group, led by one Markos. But his outline of their doctrine is thought to be of the school of Ptolemy. Their teaching has the same general shape as that of the Sethians, but with notable differences. Instead of outlandish Hebrew-sounding names we find nouns. The primary group of beings in the Fulness (*pleroma*) is the Ineffable, partnered by Silence, and Parent, partnered by Truth: from these four more emerge, Word (or Reason), Life, Man (Human being) and Church. We cannot here detail the whole system by which the Fulness is populated, the lower world brought into being, and order finally restored, but a few things should be noted.

This so-called Valentinian system is rational and biblical. Among theologians of all kinds the thinking of Plato was profoundly influential,

and in his system the visible material world is a shadow or copy of
the higher realm of mind and spirit. In Platonism, for instance, people
may change, but Man as a concept (idea) does not. Statements are of
uncertain opinions, but Truth is always the same. Plato reckoned it
wisdom to be engaged in the ultimate realities, where there is knowledge
and not just belief. Most early Christians adopted this kind of approach
to reality, holding that God had spoken to mankind from the other side,
in the prophets and finally in Jesus Christ. Sethian gnostics and Irenaeus'
Valentinians plainly thought they had such a message; and that knowing
it brought believers into contact with ultimate truth and life. But there
was a difference between the qualities and virtues which constituted the
heavenly order among the Valentinians, and the inventing or discovering
of biblical-sounding names among the Sethians. The 'Valentinian'
account differs from the Sethian in that the creator of this world is called
the 'Craftsman' ('Demiurge') not Ialtabaoth, and 'craftsman' is the very
term Plato uses for the divine being who copies the eternal ideas on
shapeless matter to create this world. The Valentinian Craftsman is not
evil, though at times misguided and incompetent, and he is ultimately
saved as the ruler of the lower realm, when Christ takes the elect and
the fallen Wisdom back to the Fulness where they belong. It has already
begun to appear that this Valentinian system is not only philosophical
or rational, but biblical. That is in keeping with what we have seen of
Valentinus himself, Ptolemy and Heracleon: their concern is to make
sense, rational and moral sense, of Scripture.

In this context one might mention *The Gospel of Truth*. Irenaeus
knew of such a work, attributed to Valentinus. The Nag Hammadi
tractate of that title is a deeply Christian meditation on how the world
came to be ignorant of God, and how with the coming of the Saviour,
the divine Word, knowledge of God is restored. It is beautifully
expressed even under the layer of Coptic translation, and replete with
biblical texts and imagery. It is not a gospel in the sense of a sort of life
of Jesus.

Given the two main lines represented by the Sethian and the
Valentinian approaches, which we can crudely distinguish as the
mythological and the philosophical, scholars have debated about which
came first. One can point to the Christianization of texts (like the
Apocryphon of John and the Sophia of Jesus Christ), and hold that the
myth came first, whether in a pagan-Iranian form or a Jewish-biblical
form, and was adopted into Christianity. In that case Valentinus and his

like civilized the mythology into something more Platonic, and
Christianized it with New Testament words and thoughts. This is the
prevailing view of, for example, Kurt Rudolph. The other view is that
the first movement was to explain Christian faith in terms of current
philosophy, with Valentinus a good example, and that this scheme was
made more exciting and interesting among disciples and adherents by
creating the mythic features of Sethian and similar systems (see Simone
Pétrement).

There were certainly Christian thinkers before Valentinus who are
usually labelled 'gnostic'. The most important was the Alexandrian
Basilides, who flourished about AD 120. His work was known and
respected by Clement of Alexandria later in the century. We know he
produced a great many books. Unfortunately his books are lost, and there
is a discrepancy between two early heresy-hunters, Irenaeus about 180
and Hippolytus after 200, about his teachings. Modern writers are still
divided as to which is right. Probably each of these ancients got a different
version from contemporary heretics. The Irenaean version has an ultimate
Father, from whom emanate Mind, Word, Prudence, Wisdom and Power,
and from Wisdom and Power a series of heavens and angels, 365 of them.
The ones at the bottom created this world and its nations, which they
oppress through their chief, the God of the Jews. The Father sends Mind
as Jesus Christ to deliver them. Notoriously Basilides denies that Christ
suffered: he exchanged places with Simon of Cyrene (Mark 15.20–21),
who was crucified while Jesus laughed (cf. Psalm 2.4). Even here the
Christian intelligence of the tradition of Basilides is apparent. Clement
records a long fragment of shrewd discussion of the problem of human
suffering (Layton pp.440–443).

Hippolytus' version is simpler, but dramatic, biblical and philosophical. Everything originates from the 'non-existent God', from whom the
world-seed comes. 'Non-existent' is a Platonic term: God is so far greater
than anything we can say of him, that even to say, 'He is,' is to demean
him. From his seed emerges a triple sonship, which corresponds to orders
of human being and of nature. This world has its own God, the Ruler of
the Seven, but above him is a higher being, the ruler of the Eight. Through
them the Gospel descends from the Non-existent, the Rulers learn the
truth, and it finally reaches the creatures below, who are sorted into their
proper kinds when all the things written in the Gospels happen. As in the
Irenaeus version, Basilides uses a fairly conventional set of letters of Paul
and gospels. So he takes the central Christian themes and weaves about

them, one way or another, his philosophical and speculative framework. Many theologians have done the same since.

With Basilides we should mention two other of the many movements in the ancient Church which became heretical as the Church moved on. One was attributed to a shipping magnate from the Black Sea port of Sinope. His name was Marcion, and he seems to have spent his great fortune promoting Christianity. In some parts of the east 'Christian' meant 'Marcionite'. Marcionites continued to be active under the Christian Empire (after Constantine, 306–337) and even after the rise of Islam in the seventh century. Marcion shared with the 'gnostic' groups a distinction between the God of this world and of the Old Testament Law, and a purer, holier and better 'alien God' who is the Father of Jesus Christ. The God of the Law is vengeful, variable and at times stupid: he is the God of the Old Testament, taken literally, who claims to do evil as well as good, hardens Pharaoh's heart to make him sin, made nasty things like mosquitoes, invented sex, and chooses favourites immorally. Jesus Christ is sent from the alien God to rescue the Creator's victims. The true Gospel consists only of a shortened version of Luke; and some letters of Paul are read, but corrected so as to get rid of good words said about Creation and the Law. Jesus' apostles got everything wrong, mixing up Jesus' message with that of the Creator, and Paul was raised up later to put them right. Marcion sticks with the Bible, though judging most of it to be a record of the disaster from which Jesus came to rescue mankind. He has no other mythology or metaphysics. His opposition to the Creator, however, extends to denying that the material order is good. Jesus could have no physical body; the stories of his birth are deleted, and he appears suddenly teaching in a synagogue, a full-grown (but only apparent) man. Marcion shares with many other early Christians an aversion from animal meat, wine, and sexual intercourse, all of which were invented by the Creator.

The last movement we should mention is rather an area than a group. East and North of Palestine Christianity spread early to Syria and beyond, into Babylonia (modern Iraq), Persia (Iran) and India. In these areas the Church language was often Syriac, a version of the Aramaic language of Palestine. In these areas Christianity took many forms which were different from those in the Greek and Latin territories of the Roman Empire to the West. Some of their traditions persisted, though they came to be generally suppressed by the official Church of the Empire. Further East, Christianity largely succumbed to persecution, first by the Parthian rulers of Persia, then by Islam; the relics which survive down to today, though they have interesting features, are largely derived from the Byzantine Church which prevailed before Islam became dominant. In the early days Marcionite Christianity was very strong. It spread East, and the last historical traces were near the Indian frontier after AD 700. In the second century Marcion was criticized by a Christian philosopher called Bardesanes (or Bardaisan), who worked and evangelized in Syria and Armenia. His work was later regarded as heretical further West.

Meanwhile the faith flourished in various forms. In particular a bilingual scholar called Tatian, who had worked in Rome about 150 and who wrote a devastating anti-pagan defence of Christianity, settled in the East and compiled an important 'harmony' of the four canonical gospels known as the Diatessaron ('Fourfold'). That became established in the Syrian churches till it was rooted out in the fifth century by ortho- dox bishops. It is lost, unfortunately, in its original Greek and Syriac forms; but the fragmentary remains do not show any convincing signs that Tatian used other than the four well-known gospels. In the Syrian churches however there were other important traditions. One was that baptism was generally regarded, as among the Marcionites, as commit- ting a person to a life of sexual abstinence: it was therefore usually deferred till late in life, and the baptized probably lived in quasi-monastic communities. They also abstained from eating flesh and drinking wine. Furthermore, their baptismal ceremonies emphasized anointing with oil rather than the washing in water.

A last characteristic worth recording is that among the Syrian Christians Thomas the Apostle, often called Judas Thomas, plays a large part. Just as in other Christian centres apostolic founders or martyrs were celebrated – Peter and Paul at Rome, John at Ephesus, James in Jerusalem, Mark in Alexandria – so Thomas was remembered by oriental Christians in Edessa and elsewhere . We looked in the last chapter at the *Acts of Thomas*. Here we note that one short treatise from Nag Hammadi, *The Book of Thomas the Contender,* depicts Judas (Jude) Thomas, the twin brother of Jesus, getting answers from Jesus before his ascension, chiefly on the fate of the wicked, and especially of those who persecute the elect. The name 'Thomas' means 'Twin' in Syriac, just as 'Didymus' does in Greek, and plainly someone in Syria answered the question, 'Whose twin was Thomas?' by identifying him with one of the brothers of Jesus. This was based on such texts as John 11.16, 14.22;

Mark 6.3, and perhaps the Epistle of Jude 'the brother of James', James being himself 'the Lord's brother'.

Of greatest interest is perhaps *The Gospel According to Thomas*. This title is attached to one of the Nag Hammadi documents, which is now included in collections of New Testament Apocrypha. The book begins, 'These are the secret words which the living Jesus spoke and Didymus Judas Thomas wrote down'. In addition to the complete Coptic copy, a fragmentary Greek papyrus from the second or third century contains parts of fourteen of the 114 or so sayings found in the later Coptic. This 'gospel' gives very little context and no attempt at continuous history. Editors number the sayings differently. A similar sayings-format would also be the form of the hypothetical sayings-source ('Q'), which many scholars suppose to lie behind stories and sayings found in both Matthew and Luke but not in Mark.

Three facts should be noticed about the opening of Thomas. First, the words are 'secret', picking up the idea that Jesus taught his disciples more than is recorded in the canonical Gospels. This is an idea often suggested in Mark (e.g. 4.10 and 4.33–34), and seized upon by 'gnostic' sects of the second century, who claimed to know secret traditions not written in the four gospels. Second, it is the 'living Jesus' who speaks these words. This sets the sayings after his resurrection, in a context like that of Luke 24.44–48, another common notion. Third, the recipient is the Twin, Judas Thomas, suggesting Syrian origin. This opening, like some of the sayings, may reflect later editorial work: many of the sayings and mini-episodes belong more naturally earlier in the life of Jesus. Neither the author's name, nor the post-resurrection setting, is likely to be original.

Over half the sayings in Thomas have parallels, some close and some loose, in the canonical NT: most parallels are to Matthew and/or Luke, about half to Mark as well, half a dozen to John, and one to 1 Corinthians 2.9. It is unlikely that these are all copied from the canonical books. Although the present text plainly contains words added or changed in the course of centuries, it is possible that some form of the collection was originally independent of the canonical gospels, and each text must be carefully examined to try to assess priority. If the author did use Matthew and Luke, he did not copy their text, but paraphrased, summarized and 'improved' it. A random example is saying 63, where the story found in Luke 12.16–21 appears as:

Jesus said, 'There was a rich man who had considerable wealth. He said, "I will use my money to sow and reap and fill my warehouses with fruit so that I will lack nothing." Such were his intentions. But in that night he died. He who has ears, let him hear.'

This short version perhaps originates as a story told by word of mouth, independent of Luke, and might go back to Jesus. One may therefore consider whether a saying like 8 contains an original reminiscence which the canonical gospels have missed:

And he said, 'Man is like a wise fisherman who cast his net into the sea. He drew it out of the sea full of small fish. The wise fisherman found among them a large, good fish. He threw all back into the sea and chose the large fish without hesitation. He who has ears to hear, let him hear.'

This combines the net, which gathers good and bad fish, of Matthew 13.47–50, with the notion of a hidden treasure, or a pearl of great price, worth more than anything else, which come just before in Matthew 13.44–45. It could represent Jesus' original use of the story of the net full of fish: not indicating the last judgment as in Matthew, but the love of God in the heart of the wise man.

The work of interpretation is complicated, as some rare biographical items show. Thomas 13 gives a version of the scene when Jesus asks his disciples who people think he is. In Mark 8.27–30 and parallels Simon Peter holds pride of place, giving the final, true answer: Jesus is the Christ. In Thomas 13 Peter speaks first, followed by Matthew, both giving inadequate answers – he is a righteous angel, or a wise philosopher. Finally, Thomas himself confesses that Jesus is beyond description, and is allowed to hear secret names. This process demotes Peter, and also Matthew, both sometimes thought to represent Jewish-Christian traditions of the primitive Church in Palestine, which we shall come upon in the next chapter. Immediately preceding however, Thomas 12 has the disciples asking Jesus, 'We know that you will go away from us; who will be our leader?' They get the answer, 'Wherever you are, go to James the just; heaven and earth came into being for him.' This James, the brother of the Lord, was the leading figure in the first Jerusalem church. In those circles this particular saying probably originated, not like the Thomas-saying which follows it. Neither episode is likely to be historically true. Each is a treasured tradition of one particular church, expressing its loyalty to a local founding father or martyr. So the Gospel of Thomas seems to combine material from different traditions and centres.

Women have a small place in Thomas. Salome, who visits Christ's tomb with Mary Magdalene in Mark 16.1, and consequently appears in some other early documents as one who receives special revelations, appears in Saying 61:

> Jesus said, 'Two will be resting on a couch; one will die, the other will live [cf. Luke 17.34].' Salome said, 'Who are you, man? [text uncertain] You have mounted my bed and have eaten from my table.' Jesus said to her, I am he who derives his being from one who is undifferentiated. The things of my Father have been given to me [Matthew 11.27 and parallel].'
>
> 'I am your disciple.'
>
> 'Therefore, I say, when he is united he will be filled with light, but if he is divided he will be filled with darkness' [Matthew 6.22–23: the eye must be single].

Here we have an explanation of the mysterious saying about two on one bed, where one will be taken and the other left. It is interpreted in terms of a spirituality of union with the invisible, superior realm, where every soul has its partner. Jesus comes with the Father's light to reunite each elect soul to his/her spiritual nature, a concept met in some 'Valentinian' texts. This of course tells us nothing about the history of Jesus or Salome. It does, however, accord with the strong ascetic preference in this Gospel for the celibate life of the monachos, the 'single one', the word which came to mean 'monk'.

In Saying 114, Mary (presumably Magdalene) appears:

> Simon Peter said to them, 'Let Mary leave us, because women are not worthy of life.' Jesus said, 'Look, I shall lead her so that I will make her male in order that she also may become a living spirit, resembling you males. For every woman who makes herself male will enter the kingdom of God.'

This is obviously not about a physical sex-change, but about a spiritual transformation. There was a presumption of male superiority among

ancient monks and ascetics generally. The idea was attributed to the
Valentinians that the female elements in both men and women were
to be 'masculinized' through union with their angelic counterparts
(see Clement of Alexandria, *Extracts from Theodotus* 21.1–3).

In summary, if we regard Thomas as an early document, possibly older
than the canonical gospels, we have in it a very early tradition of Jesus
being represented as a supernatural Wisdom figure, the introducer of
heavenly knowledge. It gives not the slightest support for the view that
the primitive Church regarded Jesus just as a superior prophet: he is
a supernatural or divine being. Most would hold that Thomas is either
a rehash of material taken from the canonical gospels, or an early
collection adapted and much developed in the sort of ascetic, spiritual
and gnostic direction found in most of the Nag Hammadi books. Even
a comparison with the Greek fragments of the same gospel shows that
the Coptic gospel has had a long history of change and development.

Our last text from Nag Hammadi is *The Gospel of Philip*. This title
is attached to a collection of paragraphs, which look like sermon
extracts, but include some sayings or short conversations of Jesus. It
has features usually associated with Valentinians. Some of them believed
that Jesus derived his body (or apparent body) through Mary from the
Craftsman add the Valentinian creator), while the Saviour descended
upon him from the Fulness at his Baptism. This may be reflected in
Saying 15, which argues that the Lord would not have spoken of his
'Heavenly Father' if he had not also had another father. Most features
however are not obviously unorthodox, featuring New Testament texts
and formulae like that of the three names, Father, Son and Holy Spirit.
Sacraments are prominent, with emphasis on their spiritual use. The
highest form of initiation is called the 'bridal chamber', in which the
soul of the elect man or woman is united as bride to her male angelic
counterpart. We know more about the meaning of the ceremony than
about what it consisted of.

Some modern readers are interested in what is said about Mary
Magdalene. Saying 28 speaks briefly of the three Marys who always kept
company with the Lord, his mother, his sister, and his 'companion' or
'partner', the Magdalene. There is also the difficult Saying 48. The text
is damaged, but it reads (Layton p.339):

The Wisdom who is called barren wisdom is the mother of the
angels. And the companion of the [...] Mary Magdalene. The

[... loved] her more than [all] the disciples, [and he used to] kiss her on her [... more] often than the rest of the [disciples...] They said to him, 'Why do you love her more than all of us?' The savior answered, saying to them, 'Why do I not love you like her? If a blind person and one with sight are both in darkness, they are not different from one another. When the light comes, the person with sight will see the light, and the blind person will remain in the darkness.'

This probably refers to kissing on the lips. But the context of that kissing is communicating truth. Unlike the debilitated 'lower wisdom', who features in some Valentinian stories as creator of the Craftsman and his angels, Mary receives pure wisdom, from the ultimate spiritual partner, Christ. She is not blind, like the disciples, so it is worthwhile bestowing light upon her. In The Second Apocalypse of James (not in Layton, but in *The Nag Hammadi Library* p.253), the risen Jesus appears to James the Just. He kisses James on the mouth while teaching him, and promises, 'My beloved, I shall reveal to you those things that neither the heavens nor the archons [Rulers] have known.' Kissing is, as with Mary, the sign of communicating to the spiritual ones a truth denied to others. Mary is not represented as the physical wife or partner, but as signifying spiritual communication. Her prominence in these sayings and in some other 'gnostic' documents may indeed indicate that there were circles in the early Church which valued the spiritual contribution of women as teachers, scholars and prophets. But that is deducible from her prominence as a witness of the resurrection of Jesus in the canonical texts, which second-century writers filled out with accounts of his post-resurrection teaching. We meet other examples among the apocryphal texts.

What does gnosticism teach us? The surviving texts and fragments of second-century Christianity suggest great creativity in thought, serious engagement with intellectual problems of getting a spiritual message from the Old Testament, a strong sense of spiritual reality and its call to transcend worldly concerns and passions, and a capacity for putting deep and complicated thoughts into marvellous, fantastic stories. We can learn a lot about ourselves from them, and about their brilliant predecessors who compiled the books of the New Testament.

Further Reading

The best single introduction is Christoph Markschies, *Gnosis: An Introduction* (T&T Clark, 2003). Very informative remains Kurt Rudolph, *Gnosis: the Nature and History of an Ancient Religion*, (translation ed. R. McL. Wilson, Continuum, 1983), but it takes a viewpoint about the origin or the system now outdated, a viewpoint shared by Hans Jonas in *The Gnostic Religion: the Message of the Alien God and the Beginnings of Christianity* (Beacon Press, 1963), and by the classic Rudolf Bultmann, *Theology of the New Testament* (S.C.M. Press, 1952). An alternative interpretation is in Simone Pétrement, *A Separate God: The Christian Origins of Gnosticism* (Harper Collins, 1990).

For the Nag Hammadi texts, see *The Nag Hammadi Library in English* (translated by members of the Coptic Gnostic Library Project of the Institute for Antiquity and Christianity, directed by James M. Robinson, Brill, 1977). With full explanatory notes is Bentley Layton, *The Gnostic Scriptures* (S.C.M. Press and Bantum USA, 1987; cited as 'Layton'). Some important texts with discussion appear in in E. Hennecke and W. Schneemelcher, *New Testament Apocrypha* (English translation ed. by R. McL. Wilson, rev. ed. James Clark, 1991; cited as 'Hennecke'), and J. K. Elliott, *The Apocryphal New Testament: A Collection of Apocryphal Christian Texts in an English translation* (Clarendon Press, 1993; cited as 'Elliott').

On the nature of heresy, classic is Walter Bauer, *Orthodoxy and Heresy in Earliest Christianity* (S.C.M. Press, 1972), and, for reference, *A Companion to Second-Century Christian 'Heretics'* (ed. Antti Marjanen and Petri Luomanen, Brill, 2005; *Supplements to Vigiliae Christianae* 76). The early chapters of Stuart G. Hall, *Doctrine and Practice in the Early Church* (SPCK, second edition, 2005) are useful. See also Bert Ehrman, *Lost Christianities* (Oxford University Press), 2003.

Chapter 6

What Was the Qumran Sect and Did Jesus Share Their Beliefs?

Stephen Need

On a recent visit to see the Dead Sea Scrolls in the Shrine of the Book at the Israel Museum in West Jerusalem I was reminded that even though Dan Brown's best-selling novel *The Da Vinci Code* is a gripping read, what it has to say about the scrolls is seriously misleading. In spite of the author's statement that his research is accurate, his claims that the scrolls were discovered in the 1950s and contain material about the human Jesus need correcting. Such inaccuracies may not affect the value of the novel, of course, but the book certainly gives a flawed impression of the real content and significance of the scrolls. Considering how popular Brown's book and the film made out of it have become, it is surely very important that the truth about the scrolls, and the Qumran sect associated with them, now be made more widely known. Of course, the media have often claimed that the scrolls reveal something sensational about Jesus and the origins of Christianity. And the idea that Jesus was a member of the sect that produced the scrolls, that he was married and divorced and fathered several children, and that all this can be found in the scrolls themselves, is nothing new with Brown's novel. It is even more important, therefore, to clarify the real facts concerning the scrolls.

The Dead Sea Scrolls were actually discovered between 1947 and 1956 and contain nothing at all about Jesus. They were very probably attached to a sect that lived in the place where they were found: Qumran on the north-western shore of the Dead Sea. It is most likely that this sect was the Essenes who are known to historians from a number of other ancient sources. There is nothing in the Dead Sea Scrolls about Jesus or his family. Indeed, there is nothing in them that tells us anything specific about the origins of Christianity as such. Although the scrolls are of considerable importance to the study of early Christianity and the world in which Jesus lived, they have nothing to do with Christianity in the ways usually claimed in the media. In fact, the Dead Sea Scrolls are Jewish texts and their greatest significance is for understanding the Judaism of the period in which they were written. Even though there are many striking parallels and similarities between the scrolls and Jesus and early Christianity, the scrolls' real significance in this respect lies in the fact that they fill in the general background to the Jewish world into which Jesus and the first Christians were born. In this essay I shall first briefly tell the story of the discovery of the Dead Sea Scrolls and give a broad outline of what they are; second, give an overview of what can be known about the Qumran sect that most probably owned the scrolls; and third, outline some features of the relation of the sect to Jesus and early Christianity. In the final section my comments will be limited largely to the first century and to material found in the gospels and the letters of St. Paul.

The Discovery of the Dead Sea Scrolls

One day, probably in the spring of 1947, a young Arab boy from one of the Bedouin tribes near the Dead Sea threw a stone in the direction of one of his goats to try to bring it back on course. He heard a resounding noise that led him to investigate what turned out to be a cave. When the boy returned later with his friends they found jars that eventually turned out to contain scrolls. Further visits revealed more caves, more jars and more scrolls. The boys decided to take their mysterious finds through the mountains of the Dead Sea area to Bethlehem to sell them at a market. The scrolls eventually landed on the stall of a Syrian Orthodox Christian who alerted his bishop in Jerusalem. The bishop then contacted the Hebrew University on Mount Scopus in Jerusalem and soon the story was out that this was the greatest discovery of biblical manuscripts ever. In the next nine years eleven caves were found in the area all containing jars with scrolls. Between 850 and 950 scrolls were represented from among thousands of fragments. In the early 1950s, Khirbet Qumran or 'the ruin of Qumran' near where the scrolls had been found was excavated. The archaeologists came from the famous École Biblique in Jerusalem and the excavations revealed the remains of a series of buildings that looked as though they had once belonged to a community. Specific rooms were identified including a dining room and a room for copying scrolls. About eleven hundred graves containing male skeletons were found in a cemetery at the site (four female skeletons whose significance remains unclear were also discovered). The archaeologists immediately made a connection between the community and a sect known as the Essenes that were already known to have lived in the area in the first century CE. It was assumed that a community that had owned the scrolls that had been found nearby had lived in the buildings and at some time, probably during the Jewish war against the Romans in 66–70 CE, had hidden their library in the caves and fled from the Romans. Indeed, although often disputed, this remains the main interpretation of the connection between the scrolls and the archaeological site. Whatever the relation was, the scrolls had been hidden in the caves at Qumran for nearly two thousand years.

To understand the Qumran sect, it is important to know something about the scrolls that were found in the caves. There are three main categories: first, scrolls of books that are known from the Hebrew Bible and apocrypha, such as the Isaiah scroll and the books of Tobit or Jubilees; second, commentaries on those books such as the Commentary on Habakkuk or Isaiah; and third, scrolls concerning the life of a community that seems to have lived somewhere in the area, such as the *Community Rule*; the *Damascus Document*; the *Messianic Rule*; the *War of the Sons of Light against the Sons of Darkness*; and the *Temple Scroll*. Across these three categories there were narratives, hymns, poetry, calendars, prayers and liturgical material, written in Hebrew, Aramaic or Greek. Copies of all the books from the Hebrew Bible were found at Qumran apart from Esther. There was also nothing of the book of Nehemiah but as this was part of the two-part Book of Ezra in the ancient world and copies of Ezra were found it is usually claimed that Nehemiah must have been known at Qumran as well. Quite a number of copies of some books were found, for example 15 copies of the Book of Genesis and 17 of the Book of Exodus. In relation to our overall interest in this essay, it is important to note that there were no scrolls of books of the New Testament found at Qumran. One or two scholars have tried to claim that some fragments of Mark's gospel and 1 Timothy were discovered there but the case for this is extremely weak. It is also worth noting that the Essenes to whom the scrolls most likely belonged are never mentioned in the New Testament. Overall, the Dead Sea Scrolls go back about a thousand years before any manuscripts of the Hebrew Bible that were known before 1947.

The Qumran Sect: Community Life and Belief

Who exactly were the sect that owned the Dead Sea Scrolls and what can be established about them? There are three sources of evidence: one is the Dead Sea Scrolls themselves; another is the archaeological excavations at

Qumran; and the third is ancient writers that refer to the sect. The
Dead Sea Scrolls themselves tell us a great deal about the community to
which they belonged and constitute the main source. The excavations at
Qumran have revealed that it is likely that the sect had its origins in the
late third or early second century BCE and continued until the Jewish war
of 66–70 CE. This was a tremendously important period in the history
of Judaism and of the region. The Qumran sect is usually identified with
the sect known as the Essenes who lived near the Dead Sea in the first
century CE and if this is correct then our third source consists of the
ancient writers Pliny the Elder, Philo of Alexandria and especially
Josephus, all of whom witness to the Essenes' existence. Not all scholars
are agreed that the Essenes and the Qumran sect are the same group, but
most think so. None of the ancient writers gives an overall view of the
Essenes but a general picture can be pieced together.

Most of the following evidence for the Qumran sect comes from the
scrolls and Josephus. It is clear from these that there were two main types
of Essene: there were those that lived in community at Qumran; and
there was an itinerant group based in the towns and villages around the
country. The first group, the Qumran sect, was unmarried, celibate, and
lived in community while the second group was married, had children
and lived out in contact with local people. The Qumran sect is usually
thought to be the home base of the whole Essene movement with the
itinerant group attached to it, although it could have been the other way
round. We do not know how many members of the community there
were at any one time and the excavations at Qumran have revealed
hardly anything that looks like residential accommodation. It is possible
that members of the sect lived in nearby caves.

From the Dead Sea Scrolls themselves, especially the *Community Rule*,
we know that the Qumran sect had a leader known as the Teacher of
Righteousness. The community was of largely priestly descent and was
hierarchical in structure: it had a governing council directing daily life
and religious practice; a Guardian that oversaw community life and
relations; and a Bursar that was responsible for money and material
possessions. The sectarians studied the Torah and Rule, worked on the
land in agriculture and farming, and held a regular meal that formed
the focus of community life. Initiation into the sect took place in stages
over two or three years. There were two basic steps: first, entering the
Covenant; and second, entering the community. Anyone wishing to
enter the sect would appear before the council for consideration. Once

accepted, they swore obedience to the Torah and the Rule. There was then still another year before the person was completely admitted. At this point he handed over his money and possessions and could then speak in the Council. Just how strict the sect was is indicated in a series of rules which, if broken, could result in an appropriate punishment. This sometimes involved dismissal from the community. For example, taking the divine name in vain; speaking against the community or the Rule; lying to the community; disrespect to community members; rudeness; insulting behaviour; anger; going naked unnecessarily; not caring for a member; spitting; falling asleep during a council meeting; and 'guffawing foolishly' in the council, could all result in a penance, discipline or dismissal. Sometimes members of the sect were excluded from the community meal for a season. Archaeological excavations at Qumran have added to this picture. A significant number of 'immersion pools' (Hebrew: *miqva'ot*) have been discovered indicating that in common with other Jews of the second temple period members of the sect passed through water as a way of marking out the various activities of their day and keeping 'purity' in relation to the Torah.

The second group, the itinerant Essenes, were rather different from the group based at Qumran. They had a much more flexible and independent existence. They lived in towns and villages and moved around the land freely. They were married, had children and lived with their families, although there were rules to be kept, for example about sexual relations. They had jobs and mixed with the Gentile population. There was less of an emphasis on the strict observance of the Torah although people could be dismissed for not conforming. There was no initiation process and members of the group kept their own property. Like the Qumran group they had a Guardian that guided relations with outsiders. They did have meetings but there was no council as such. There was no common meal as at Qumran and it seems to have been acceptable for them to worship in the Temple at Jerusalem.

The religious beliefs of the Qumran sect are crucial to our assessment of their relation to Jesus and early Christianity. As Jews of the second temple period there are a number of things that they definitely believed and these are clear from the scrolls: they believed in the one God of the Jews and in the Covenant and Torah. These were the foundations of all Jewish belief. They also concentrated on interpreting the Torah and other authoritative texts specifically for their own time. In this sense prophecy and biblical interpretation were central, as indicated by the commentaries on biblical books found in the caves at Qumran. The members of the sect saw themselves as the true Israel and as the new Covenant people. They saw themselves as the chosen ones through whom God was working out his purpose for Israel. They believed that the world was divided between those who were members of the sect and those who were not. It is highly likely that the Qumran sect was an extremist group that had gone to the Dead Sea area in order to escape the Jerusalem Temple and its sacrificial system. No evidence of sacrifice has been found at Qumran and it looks as though this was an anti-Temple sect that had left Jerusalem (where there is also archaeological evidence of Essenes) and gone to the desert to live a more rigorous life. Their Qumran scroll entitled *The War of the Sons of Light Against the Sons of Darkness* indicates that they saw the world in radically dualistic terms, that is they believed that there were two basic forces in the universe, light and darkness, good and evil, and that at the end of time (which would be soon) there would be a cosmic battle between the two sides. They also believed that two messiahs would come, a priestly messiah and a kingly messiah. Further evidence indicates that they believed in resurrection and immortality. All these beliefs defined their basic outlook and daily practice.

One feature of the Qumran sect that has a significant parallel in the lives of Jesus and the early Christians is the communal meal they shared. There is evidence for this at Qumran from Josephus and Philo, from the scrolls themselves, and also from the possible remains of a dining room at the site. The scrolls do not say how frequently the meal was held but Josephus indicates twice a day, morning and afternoon. He also says that a special bath was taken beforehand and special garments were put on. Ten men were to be gathered in the presence of a priest. There were no women. Everyone was to be seated in order of rank and importance. The meal was to begin with a prayer (Josephus and the scrolls) and end with one (Josephus). The scrolls indicate that prayer was said over the bread and wine although it is possible that there was other food at the meal as well. There is a reference to 'new wine' which might indicate wine with low alcohol for ascetic reasons. It is unclear whether there was meat at the meal but animal bones have been found at Qumran along with eating pots. Access to the meal was based on being initiated into the sect and on staying in. If rules were broken a member could be excluded from the meal. It is clear that the meal had messianic and eschatological signific-ance to the community; it played a key part in the sect's sense of purity and was central to its daily life.

From the various sources it can be seen that the Qumran sect probably was indeed the Essenes, an ascetic, religious group that lived a contemplative life in a community near the north-western shore of the Dead Sea around the time of Jesus. They kept the Torah strictly and interpreted it in relation to their own destiny. It is important to note here that there is nothing else quite like the Qumran sect in ancient Judaism or indeed in any Judaism. The sect certainly looks like a later Christian monastic community and there is something to be learnt from seeing it in this light although one must be cautious of making too much of this analogy.

Qumran, Jesus and Early Christianity

When we turn to consider the relation of the Qumran sect to Jesus and early Christianity some obvious questions arise: did Jesus know the Qumran sect and was he influenced by it in any way? Were the early Christians influenced by it? Was St. Paul, the first great Christian theologian, influenced by this sect? Before looking at any of these questions, however, there is another: was John the Baptist, the forerunner of Jesus, related to the Qumran sect in any way? This is a question that has occupied scholars since the early days of scrolls scholarship and a small number have concluded that John did indeed belong to the Qumran sect. However, most scholars now conclude that there is simply not enough evidence for us to be sure of this.

In the New Testament gospels, John the Baptist is the forerunner of Jesus. He preaches his own message of repentance for the forgiveness of sins and baptizes with water in distinction from Jesus' baptism in the Holy Spirit (Mark 1.1–8). The water baptism raises the question whether John might have been a member of the Qumran sect as they took part so much in water rituals. Was John a member of the sect or at least of the itinerant group? Was he an Essene or had he been one at some stage of his life? There are other things that point to a possible connection here too. John came from a priestly family; he was the son of Zechariah the priest (Luke 1.5); he operated in the desert (Luke 1.80); and baptized people in the region of 'Bethany across the Jordan' (Luke 1.28) and 'in the region of Aenon near Salim' (John 3.23). It is not really clear where these places were but they were probably somewhere near the southern end of the River Jordan in the Dead Sea area not far from Qumran. John is presented in the gospels as an individual like Elijah, a prophetic figure from the Jewish past that was to return at the end of time. An interest in prophecy is very strong in the Dead Sea Scrolls and John the Baptist is introduced in the gospels with a quotation from the Book of Isaiah (Mark 1.2), an important prophetic book, copies of which were found at Qumran. It is also interesting to note, furthermore, that as far as we know John the Baptist was probably celibate; it would make a lot of sense if he belonged to the Qumran sect.

In spite of all this, however, it cannot be concluded definitely that John the Baptist did have connections with Qumran at the time of Jesus' ministry or had ever done so. All of these characteristics could have been true of many people of the time and they do not add up to enough evidence to say with certainty that John belonged to the sect. The most that can be said is that he might have done so. In any case, one important conclusion can be reached here: John the Baptist came from the same Jewish world as the members of the Qumran sect. Given this common background it is inevitable that they drew upon the same stock of lan-guage and ideas and held many beliefs and practices in common. It can already be seen from this that the Dead Sea Scrolls and the Qumran sect are a very important part of the background not only to John but also to Jesus and the early Christians.

The next question is whether Jesus was connected to the Qumran sect or influenced by it in any way. A prior question must be: 'what do we know about Jesus that can be compared to what we know about the Qumran sect?' It is important to remember here that the four New Testament gospels are our only source for the historical Jesus and they were written years after his lifetime by people who believed that he had fulfilled God's ancient promises to the Jews. We must therefore think of 'Jesus and early Christianity' together here as it is not always clear whether material in the four gospels comes from Jesus or from the writers themselves. Even so, we know from the fact that Jesus was a Jew that he would have believed in the same basic things as the members of the Qumran sect simply because he came from broadly the same Jewish world as them. Like members of the Qumran sect he clearly believed in the one God of the Jews, in the Covenant that God established with his people Israel, and in the Torah. As we have seen, the Qumran sectarians were keen on interpreting scripture and read much of it as referring to themselves. They saw their own sect as members of the new Covenant who were fulfilling the ancient prophecies of Israel. From the New Testament it is also clear that the gospel writers saw Jesus as one who had fulfilled Jewish prophecy. For them Jesus was the one who was baptized by John the Baptist; who preached a gospel of repentance; who interpreted scripture to people; and who preached the coming of a new age. It looks as though Jesus himself envisaged a new community connected to the end of time and it is possible that he saw himself in messianic terms too.

There are also other elements that Jesus, the early Christians and the Qumran sect had in common. Like most Jews of his day, Jesus believed in two distinct ages, the present age and the age to come; in a world of good and evil; in the basic sinfulness of human beings; and in God's offer of forgiveness and salvation to his people. Basic features of Jewish practice might also look as though they connect Jesus to Qumran, for example an emphasis on prayer (Matthew 6.5f) and on issues of purity relating to food (Mark 7.1f). There is also the question of the water rituals that characterized the Qumran sect and John the Baptist. To what extent might Jesus be connected to water rituals through his baptism by John? More specifically, Jesus encouraged his disciples to share or give up their possessions (Luke 10.4f) and also condemned divorce (Matthew 5.31–32). His critical attitude to the Temple in the gospels (e.g. Mark 11.15–19) and his emphasis on ethical purity (e.g. Matthew 5) also tie in with the ideals of the Qumran sect. Another thing that has caused a great deal of speculation is Jesus' apparent celibacy and exhortation to celibacy (Matthew 19.12). This was unusual for a Jew of his day but the Qumran sect was a community of celibate males. Does this indicate that Jesus knew the sect or was influenced by it? All these features align Jesus with some of the central beliefs and practices of the Qumran sect as we know it from the main sources. But even though this indicates a common religious world view and set of practices it does not necessarily establish a clear historical connection between Jesus or the gospel writers and Qumran.

Probably the most significant parallel between Jesus, early Christianity and the Qumran sect is the 'Last Supper' meal that Jesus celebrated with his disciples the night before the crucifixion and that the early Christians took up as their main ritual celebration. Meals are important in Jesus' ministry especially in the gospel of Luke and the 'Last Supper' is the main one. From the four gospels and St. Paul's first letter to the Corinthians we know that Jesus shared a meal with his disciples the night before he died. Scholars have debated whether this was a Jewish Passover meal or some other sort of meal. In the Gospels of Matthew, Mark, and Luke, although the accounts differ, the meal is most likely a Passover meal commemorating the freeing of the people of Israel from slavery in Egypt. In John's gospel the dating of the meal is different: it is certainly not a Passover meal because Jesus dies at the very moment that the Passover lambs are being sacrificed in preparation for the feast. This difference in John's gospel could have arisen for symbolic, theological reasons, but it is also possible that the community that wrote this gospel operated on a different calendar from the rest of Judaism, a solar calendar. It so happens that the Qumran sect operated on a solar calendar rather than the lunar calendar of mainstream Judaism and the Jerusalem Temple. Some scholars have concluded that this shows a strong link between St. John's Gospel and the Qumran sect. As far as the meal itself is concerned, it is clear that both Jesus and the Qumran sect valued meals and table fellowship generally. For both, the meal was associated with the coming of the messiah and with the end of time. In spite of these parallels, however, the Qumran sect and Jesus and the early Christians had different attitudes to their meals: at Qumran, if the rules of the community were broken, members could be excluded, whereas the Christian meal was much more inclusive at least in intention (though see Matthew 22.11–14).

In spite of differences there are other similarities to be taken into account. Of course, Jesus spoke Aramaic and his words in the gospels are in Greek. It is not, therefore, advisable simply to draw straight lines from the gospels, to Qumran, to Jesus. Even so, echoes in the use of language and even obvious differences could imply some connection between Jesus or the gospel writers and the Qumran sect. Expressions used in the gospels such as the 'sons of light' (Luke 16.8) and the 'Son of the Most High' (Luke 1.32) are found in the scrolls (the first in the *Community Rule* and the second in an Aramaic Apocryphon of Daniel). There was no evidence of the latter expression anywhere in ancient Jewish literature until it was found at Qumran. There are also a lot of parallels between the scrolls and the Sermon on the Mount (Matthew 5–7) and a series of Beatitudes have been found in a Qumran scroll known as 4QBeatitudes. Some scholars think that Jesus or the gospel writers could have been reacting against the teachings of Qumran on some occasions. For example when Jesus tells his disciples to love their enemies (Matthew 5.43f) he might have been reacting against an injunction in the *Community Rule* to hate outsiders and enemies. Such material often looks as though it establishes a firm connection between Jesus or the gospel writers and the Qumran sect but the evidence is ultimately inconclusive.

One major difference between Jesus and the Qumran sectarians appears if we take the way Jesus is portrayed overall in the gospels: he clearly has a very different lifestyle from the members of the Qumran sect. In the gospels Jesus is a frequenter of dinner parties, drinking wine and mixing with different types of people. He is at ease with the outcast, lepers, women, prostitutes and others, and is quite unlike the members of the Qumran sect who are more akin to an exclusive monastic community. Jesus' overall lifestyle and sense of direction is quite different from that of those who belonged to the Qumran sect.

In considering the question of the relation between the Qumran sect and early Christianity it is important not to omit the letters of St. Paul. Paul was the first and most important of the early Christian theologians. He wrote letters to Christian communities around the Mediterranean world and although he mostly operated well away from Qumran itself much of his mindset was still rooted in the Judaism of his day. Although his theology focused on Jesus Christ and in that sense was very different from the Qumran sect, Paul nevertheless used language and concepts that came from a Jewish world common to them both. Two very interesting examples here come from Paul's famous theology of 'justification'. In his letters to the Romans and the Galatians he writes frequently about 'the righteousness of God' (e.g. Romans 1.17) and 'the works of the Law' (e.g. Galatians 2.16). These two expressions are well known to Christian theologians and of course the subjects of righteousness and the Law are everywhere in ancient Judaism. But the actual expressions Paul uses never appear in the Hebrew Bible and scholars have often wondered where they came from and whether they were Paul's own. Since the Dead Sea Scrolls were discovered the two expressions have been found (the first in the *Community Rule* and the second in *Some Precepts of the Torah*) showing that Paul was using language already current in first-century Judaism. This does not change the content of Paul's theology, of course, and certainly does not mean that Paul lived at Qumran! It simply helps fill in the background to Paul's thinking in a minor but significant way.

There are other elements that seem to hint at a connection between Qumran, Jesus and early Christianity. Some early Christians shared their possessions and held all things in common (Acts 2.44–45; 4.32; 5.1–11) just like the Qumran sect. Paul also encourages this in his first letter to the Corinthians (16.2). Some scholars have thought that this indicates a clear connection between Qumran and the early Christians but the cases are rather different. Members of the Qumran sect were required to give up possessions and live a common life whereas the Christians chose to do so of their own free will. Another feature of life in the Qumran sect that is often compared to the life of the early Christians is that the sect had a Guardian to oversee the practices of the community. The early Christians also came in due course to have overseers that governed their communities (1 Timothy 3). But again, although there is a broad similarity here, the cases are different. As far as Jesus and his disciples were concerned there was little hierarchy or rank in their community although from at least the second century onwards a structured system did develop in Christianity with a threefold ministry of bishops, priests and deacons. Finally, the question of celibacy comes to mind once again when we find Paul claiming that it is better to remain single than to marry (1 Corinthians 7). This is another interesting parallel with the Qumran sect but it cannot be claimed that this indicates a direct connection. It is interesting to note here that celibacy developed in later Christianity as a monastic and clerical ideal in communities that might have been very much like the one at Qumran.

The question of the relation of Jesus and the early Christians to the sect that lived at Qumran is complex and multilayered. It is not always easy to know whether we are dealing with Jesus or early Christianity when we read the New Testament gospels. For this reason, scholars have varied a great deal in their assessment of the evidence but it looks highly unlikely that Jesus himself was attached to the Qumran sect. He could certainly have known it and even visited it but the overall gospel picture of Jesus is of a very different type of figure. In fact, it is more likely that Jesus was influenced in a general way by the itinerant Essenes than by the sect that lived at Qumran. Of course, it remains possible that Jesus, the gospel writers and other early Christians including St. Paul were all influenced by the Qumran sect but it is certainly not easy to discern such influence clearly. From all the material available to us it is very difficult to establish beyond doubt any more than a common background of Jewish language, belief and practice.

Conclusion

In conclusion, we have seen that the Dead Sea Scrolls found at Qumran have nothing to do with Jesus and contain no references to him. The majority of scholars are clear that no texts from the New Testament were found among the Qumran scrolls. Readers of works like *The Da Vinci*

Code who are serious about historical matters must, therefore, beware.
The Dead Sea Scrolls are Jewish texts that reveal a great deal about
the Judaism of the period in which they were written. In conjunction
with other ancient writers and assuming that they all refer to the same
community, the scrolls reveal that the Qumran sect was an ascetic,
religious community that lived by the Dead Sea. They were a group
of celibate, contemplative men who saw themselves as members of the
new Covenant and of the true Israel. They believed, like all Jews of the
period, in the one God of the Jews and in the Covenant and the Torah
and in the interpretation of scripture for their own day. They also
believed in the imminent coming of the end of time. They were governed
by a hierarchy of leaders and shared a common meal. They were most
probably the Essenes.

There is no doubt that the parallels between the Qumran sect, Jesus
and early Christianity are striking. John the Baptist came from the same
Jewish world and believed many of the same things as the Qumran sect.
He preached a message of repentance for the forgiveness of sins and took
part in water rituals, but there is no conclusive evidence that he ever
belonged to the sect. There are also parallels with Jesus: he lived in the
same religious world as the Qumran sectarians and those that wrote
about him saw him as the messiah who established a new community
focused on the end of time. Sayings in the gospels, whether from Jesus
or the gospel writers, ring bells in the Dead Sea Scrolls and *vice versa*.
Perhaps the most striking parallel is the 'Last Supper' meal that Jesus
established with his disciples the night before he died and that was taken
up by the early Christians and held regularly thereafter as their main
religious celebration. There are numerous other minor parallels and
overlaps between the Qumran sect and Jesus or the early Christians,
for example in the Sermon on the Mount and in the language and
expressions used by St. Paul. In the end, however, none of these parallels
establishes a direct causal relation of influence between the Qumran
sect, Jesus and early Christianity. They simply demonstrate that in
spite of differences, members of the Qumran sect, Jesus and the early
Christians shared a basic religious world view and on occasions used
similar concepts and language or partook in similar practices. This was
inevitable given their common background. There may have been direct
reactions or influences of a minor sort when Jesus or the gospel writers
reacted to the teaching of the Qumran sect, or when Paul used an
expression or two that the Qumran sect also used. But it is very difficult

to establish more than a general loose relation. In the end, the importance of the Qumran sect and of the Dead Sea Scrolls for the study of Jesus and early Christianity is that they help fill in the background to the world of second temple Judaism into which Jesus and early Christianity were born; nothing more and nothing less.

Further Reading

The best way to approach the Dead Sea Scrolls is by reading Timothy H. Lim, *The Dead Sea Scrolls: A Very Short Introduction* (Oxford University Press, 2005). This gives an overview of the history and interpretation of the scrolls and includes brief discussions of most of the issues that arise in studying them. After that, Philip R. Davies, George J. Brooke and Phillip R. Callaway, *The Complete World of the Dead Sea Scrolls* (Thames and Hudson, 2002) provides a lavishly illustrated introduction to the discovery and significance of the scrolls.

The texts of the scrolls themselves are available in English with a very useful Introduction in Geza Vermes, *The Complete Dead Sea Scrolls in English* (Penguin, 2004, revised ed.). The most recent detailed scholarly study of the scrolls is a collection of essays by George J. Brooke entitled *The Dead Sea Scrolls and the New Testament* (SPCK, 2005). This includes essays on the relation between the scrolls and the New Testament generally and between the scrolls and particular texts in the New Testament. A very useful collection of essays by various scrolls scholars is James H. Charlesworth (ed.), *Jesus and the Dead Sea Scrolls* (Doubleday, 1992). This includes discussions of the historical Jesus, Qumran and archaeology.

Chapter 7
How Did the Early Christians Worship?

Graham Gould

In modern Christianity 'worship' covers a wide range of activities which could appear to an uninformed observer to have little in common – from the least formal meeting of a house church or university Christian Union to the carefully rehearsed musical performance of an Anglican cathedral evensong or the complex wording and ceremonial of an Eastern Orthodox liturgy (and many points between these different extremes). Closer or better informed investigation might reveal that these different forms of worship in fact share a number of common features, including (on most occasions) the reading of Scripture and its exposition by a qualified person, prayer of various sorts (intercession, praise, thanksgiving), and the cultivation of a sense of fellowship among those present; but the diversity of forms remains a not infrequent cause of misunderstandings among Christians and occasionally, even today, of disagreement and hostility.

It is often suggested that in the early church a change took place from the informal and spontaneous worship of the New Testament to the formal and regulated worship of later centuries. This theory is supported by considerable evidence, but the overall picture is complex, and it by no means follows that all of the characteristics of Christian worship as it was conducted from (say) the fourth century onwards were deviations from the practices of earlier centuries.

Most of this chapter will be devoted to the evidence for the way in which the eucharist (i.e. Lord's Supper, Holy Communion, or mass) was celebrated in the early church and for the early development of some of the doctrines about the eucharist which had most influence on later Christian thought. As in the chapter on the Papacy, the focus will be mainly on evidence from before the time of Constantine, with the changes of the fourth century outlined only in a much more general way. Besides the formalization of worship compared with New Testament times, one other theory that will be considered briefly is that Christianity, especially from the time of Constantine, when conversions increased and worship changed rapidly in the face of growing numbers, borrowed some of its ideas about the eucharist or its liturgical customs from contemporary paganism. This too has some truth in it, as will be explained at the end of this chapter.

The eucharist may be defined as the sharing of bread and wine by Christians in recollection of the Last Supper which, according to the first three gospels, Jesus celebrated with his disciples on the night before he died (Matthew 26.26–29, Mark 14.22–25, Luke 22.14–20). The word 'eucharist' is from the Greek term for 'thanksgiving'; its specialized use derives from the 'eucharistic' prayer, of thanksgiving or blessing, which is said over the bread and wine before they are consumed. 'Eucharist' was used in this sense in Christian writings from the early second century onwards, but not in the New Testament. The New Testament evidence for the eucharist, apart from the Last Supper narratives, is in fact quite slight, though Paul in 1 Corinthians 10.16–22 and 11.17–34 supplies important (if limited) evidence for the earliest forms of celebration.

Not all Christian worship was centred on the eucharist; quite apart from other liturgies, notably baptism and ordination (which it is not possible to consider within the confines of a brief chapter), early Christian worship, as in modern times, included besides the sharing of bread and wine elements such as prayer and praise, readings from the Scripture, and preaching. In order not to overlook these, a good place to start, before moving to the more specific evidence for the eucharist, is with two general descriptions of Christian worship written in the second century. The first of these is from a non-Christian Roman writer, Pliny the Younger, in the context of a letter about the treatment of Christians by the Roman authorities, written to the Emperor Trajan *c.*112 when Pliny was governor of the province of Bithynia (in modern Turkey):

> They maintained... that it was their habit on a fixed day to
> assemble before daylight and recite by turns a form of words to
> Christ as a god; and that they bound themselves with an oath, not
> for any crime, but not to commit theft or robbery or adultery, not
> to break their word, and not to deny a deposit when demanded.
> After this was done, their custom was to depart, and to meet again
> to take food, but ordinary and harmless food; and even this, they
> said, they had given up doing after the issue of my edict by which...
> I had forbidden the existence of clubs.
> *Epistle* 10.96

The mention of the prohibition of clubs here illustrates the Roman authorities' fear of subversive organizations, but Pliny had found the Christian meetings to be free of political danger. The reference to the oath suggests that the worship Pliny had heard about included prayer in response to a sermon or moral exhortation, perhaps based on a list of rules such as the Ten Commandments ('prayer' and 'oath' are closely related words in Greek, which these Christians would have spoken, though Pliny wrote about them in Latin). This moral emphasis in worship makes sense as a development of the exhortations which we find in the letters of Paul (e.g. Romans 12) and elsewhere in the New Testament.

The second description is from Tertullian, a theologian of Carthage in North Africa who was the first major Latin Christian writer and one of the most important theologians of the pre-Constantinian church. Tertullian's account comes in the context of his *Apology* or defence of Christianity, written *c*.197. Tertullian was concerned to show both that Christians were good citizens and that Christianity was superior to pagan religious cults, so he gives an understandably glowing account of what Christians do:

> We are a body with a common religious feeling, unity of discipline, a common bond of hope. We meet in gathering and congregation to approach God in prayer, massing our forces to surround him. This violence that we do him pleases God. We pray also for emperors, for their ministers and those in authority, for the security of the world, for peace on earth, for postponement of the end. We meet to read the books of God... There is, besides, exhortation in our gatherings, rebuke, divine censure... Certain tested elders preside, men who have reached this honour not for a price, but by character.
> *Apology*, 39

After this highly rhetorical description of a meeting for prayer, Scripture-reading, and preaching, Tertullian goes on to explain that Christians do not charge for attendance at their assembly but that all contribute voluntarily what they can afford, and to describe the common meal of the community as one of moderation and piety, without excessive drinking and concluded by prayer (in contrast, Tertullian thinks, to the meals of pagan cults).

Whether, like Pliny, Tertullian implies that the common meal was separate from the main meeting for worship and teaching is a little difficult to say, but we can probably infer that like those known to Pliny, Tertullian's Christians met twice in the day (probably Sunday), first for a service of worship and then later for a common or fellowship meal (the term often used by scholars is *agape*). This pattern is clearer but also different from what we find in the New Testament, where gatherings for worship were probably usually in the evening, though other times of the day are also possible (the meeting of the apostles at Pentecost, in Acts 2, took place in the morning), and probably varied in their nature, though the sharing of a common meal could certainly be included (cf. Jude 12). In Acts 2:42, 46 and 20:7 one of the purposes for which Christians met is described as 'breaking bread'.

From the evidence of Acts it is usually assumed that in the earliest church the common meal shared by Christians and the eucharist were identical – or, more strictly, that the eucharist was a particular set of actions, the blessing and sharing of bread and wine, that took place during a meal (on the model of the Last Supper). Pliny's evidence is (naturally enough) unspecific about the relationship between eucharist and common meal, but we know from other sources that by the early second century the two had usually become separated. How this occurred is not entirely clear, but it was one of the first steps on the way to a more formal pattern of worship. Even Paul (1 Corinthians 11.34) could recommend that the meal-aspect of the eucharist could be reduced and people encouraged to eat at home instead if the common meal was leading to arguments. But the most important factor may have been the transfer of the eucharist to early on Sunday morning, perhaps because this was believed to be the hour of the resurrection, and so that Christians could attend before starting work, while the common meal remained at a normal meal-time. Tertullian does not mention the eucharist explicitly in his *Apology* – perhaps because he thought the idea too difficult to explain in a work addressed to a pagan audience – but references elsewhere in his writings clearly show that it was received before daybreak.

Not all of the evidence from earlier in the second century agrees with this picture. A document called the *Didache* ('teaching'), a work of moral instruction and guidelines for worship, almost certainly written well before 150 and maybe as early as the first century, still presupposes that the eucharist takes place in the context of a proper meal. It includes prayers of blessing over the cup of wine and the bread which are similar in form to the prayers which Jews (including Jesus) would have used at meals, though they have been Christianized by the introduction of references to Jesus and the church (*Didache*, chs 9–10). Probably these prayers are the work of Jewish Christians whose ideas about the eucharist depended directly on their knowledge of the sort of meals which Jesus would have shared with his disciples. In the past, scholars who were worried by the absence from the prayers of the *Didache* of features which later came to be treated as essential to the eucharist, such as commemoration of the death and resurrection of Jesus or quotation of the words of institution ('this is my body' etc.) used by him at the Last Supper, reacted by suggesting that the author of the *Didache* was describing not a eucharist but an *agape*. But the explicit use of the word 'eucharist' in the instruction 'concerning the eucharist, give thanks in this way' (ch.9) makes this theory difficult to sustain: even if the author was recommending prayers which he had found in an earlier source, *he* interpreted them as eucharistic rather than connected with an *agape* – or, more likely, made no explicit distinction between the two. What scholars who took this view failed to acknowledge was that in this early period, where the eucharist was still part of a common meal, there was no fixed form of eucharistic prayer, and that probably not everyone thought that following the example of Jesus at the Last Supper required his words to be explicitly quoted.

This observation underlines the fact that diversity of form and of language in the prayers used at the eucharist – as in other aspects of worship – must have been usual in second-century Christianity. Apart from the influence of the Gospels and Paul's letters, which were gradually coming to be regarded as authoritative, there was no means by which the practices of different Christian groups, widely scattered throughout the Roman empire, could have been made to conform to one another in every detail. Nonetheless, during the later second and early third centuries, something like a pattern of eucharistic practice does begin to emerge. Our sources for this period include Justin Martyr, whose *First Apology* (written, probably in Rome, *c*.152 or shortly afterwards) contains the most detailed description of Christian worship supplied by a second-century author, and an anonymous document called the *Apostolic Tradition*, probably also from Rome from early in the third century and attributed by many scholars (though on the basis of uncertain evidence) to the theologian Hippolytus. Further details are supplied by Irenaeus of Lyons and other writers, but it must again be emphasized that in this context only a selective survey is possible.

Unlike Tertullian a generation later (if the comment above is correct) Justin did not feel any reticence about referring to the eucharist in a work addressed to a pagan audience. His main description refers to the eucharist immediately following baptism, at which newly baptized Christians would receive communion for the first time. Following the baptism itself (which seems to have been a partly private ceremony attended only by a few people), the newly baptized person is brought into the congregation, prayers of intercession are said, and a kiss of peace is exchanged among those present. Then bread, wine, and water (the water either to mix with the wine or to be drunk separately as a symbol of purity) are brought to the one who presides, who prays and gives thanks to God 'at some length that we have been deemed worthy of these things from him', after which the elements are distributed to the people by 'those whom we call deacons' (*First Apology*, 65). Justin follows this account with a short description of the Sunday eucharist (he seems to be the first Christian writer to use the pagan term Sunday rather than the Christian 'the Lord's day'). Here the service begins with readings from the Scriptures and a sermon by the one who presides, then continues with prayers and the offering of the bread and wine as at the baptismal eucharist (*First Apology*, 67). Justin notes that the deacons take the bread and wine to any who are not present.

In the *Apostolic Tradition* (ch.21) the baptismal eucharist is described in similar terms to Justin: prayer, the kiss of peace, the presentation of the bread and wine, the thanksgiving, and the distribution. As well as bread, wine, and water, a cup of milk mixed with honey is included as a symbol of blessing. But the *Apostolic Tradition* also provides an account of the eucharist in the context of an ordination service – the first description of such an event to survive. Here the newly ordained bishop leads the eucharist, and, although the author does not think that the bishop must use exactly the words that he provides, he gives an example of a eucharistic prayer which it is worthwhile to quote in full:

The deacons shall present the offering [of bread and wine by the worshippers] to him; and he, laying his hands on it with all the presbyters, shall give thanks, saying:

The Lord be with you
and all shall say:
and with your spirit.

Up with your hearts.
We have them with the Lord.
Let us give thanks to the Lord.
It is fitting and right.

And then he shall continue thus:

We render thanks to you, O God, through your beloved child
Jesus Christ, whom in the last times you sent to us as a saviour and
redeemer and angel of your will; who is your inseparable Word,
through whom you made all things, and in whom you were well
pleased. You sent him from heaven into a virgin's womb; he was
made flesh and was manifested as your Son, being born of the Holy
Spirit and the Virgin. Fulfilling your will and gaining for you a holy
people, he stretched out his hands when he should suffer, that he
might release from suffering those who have believed in you.

And when he was betrayed to voluntary suffering that he might
destroy death, and break the bonds of the devil, and tread down
hell, and shine upon the righteous, and fix a term, and manifest the
resurrection, he took bread and gave thanks to you, saying 'Take,
eat; this is my body, which shall be broken for you'. Likewise also
the cup, saying, 'This is my blood, which is shed for you; when you
do this, you make my remembrance'.

Remembering therefore his death and resurrection, we offer to
you the bread and the cup, giving you thanks because you have
held us worthy to stand before you and minister to you.

And we ask that you would send your Holy Spirit upon the offering of your holy church; that, gathering her into one, you would
grant to all who receive the holy things to receive the fulness of the
Holy Spirit for the strengthening of faith in truth; that we may praise
and glorify you through your child Jesus Christ; through whom
be glory and honour to you, to the Father and Son, with the Holy
Spirit, in your holy Church, both now and to the ages of ages. Amen.
Apostolic Tradition, 4

Presumably the distribution of the bread and wine followed immediately
after this.

If this prayer really is a third-century composition (which has been
much disputed by scholars, but is still quite plausible), it indicates the

relatively early origin of some features of the eucharistic prayer which have remained part of the usage of many Christian churches until the present day, for example the introductory dialogue between celebrant and people (which is also found in other third-century sources), the quotation of Jesus' words of institution, the offering of the bread and cup to God in the context of recalling Jesus' death and resurrection, and the closing prayer for the Holy Spirit to make the reception of the bread and wine (representative of the church which offers them) fruitful for those present. We cannot, however, be certain whether the *Apostolic Tradition* is typical of its date, or when these features became normal in all eucharistic prayers, as the evidence remains very sparse before the end of the fourth century. It is also worth noting that some features which are usually included in later eucharistic prayers are absent, particularly the quotation of the hymn from Isaiah 6 known as the *Sanctus*: 'Holy, Holy, Holy is the Lord of hosts'. (Modern worshippers in the Catholic, Anglican, and other traditions may well find the eucharistic prayer of the *Apostolic Tradition* has a familiar feel to it: this is because of its popularity as a model for the writing of new eucharistic prayers during the second half of the twentieth century.)

Justin and the *Apostolic Tradition*, then, provide us with some indications of how the eucharist was celebrated, at least in Rome. (The fact that Justin had travelled widely before settling there means that the evidence is not necessarily as geographically limited as might first appear; Hippolytus, if he was the author of the *Apostolic Tradition*, was also probably an easterner in origin.) It is perhaps difficult to evaluate the degree of formality involved in these celebrations compared with the impression given by the brief descriptions of worship which we find in the New Testament or Pliny: much would depend on the context (probably still a house-church or perhaps a hired room), the size of the gathering, and the identity and personality of the celebrant. There is a little more detail in the *Apostolic Tradition* than in Justin about the way in which the bishop and other clergy should distribute the bread and wine, water, and milk to the people, which may imply that the author envisages a larger community than Justin, around three quarters of a century before. In Justin's time the celebrant was expected to pray the eucharistic prayer in his own words; by the time of the *Apostolic Tradition*, although this was still possible, a form of words is provided, both for the eucharistic prayer and for the distribution of the bread and wine, which gradually became more fixed as the centuries wore on.

And whereas Justin uses the unspecific term 'the one who presides' (who, as was noted in the chapter on the Papacy, was not necessarily the bishop of the city), the *Apostolic Tradition* is explicit that the bishop presides and teaches the people the meaning of what is being done.

As well as these indications about eucharistic practice, second-century sources provide us with evidence for the emergence of some of the doctrines typical of later thinking about the eucharist. The most important of these is the growing confidence of Christian writers about identifying the bread and wine of the eucharist with Jesus' body and blood. The language of the New Testament (both the gospels and Paul in 1 Corinthians 10.16) can be explained as symbolic or sacramental: the bread and wine represent or make present the body and blood of Jesus as a spiritual reality, so that the meaning of the eucharist is to point to Christians' sharing in the effects of Jesus' death on the cross – being saved or becoming members of 'the new covenant in my blood' (1 Corinthians 11.25; cf. Mark 14.24). In later writings too, the bread and wine continue to be referred to as symbols or even 'likenesses' of the body and blood of Jesus (this term is found, for example, in the account of the baptismal eucharist in the *Apostolic Tradition*); but, alongside the language of symbolism, a 'realist' language of identification takes hold and becomes increasingly common.

Thus Ignatius of Antioch writes that docetic Christians (who denied that Jesus was a real human being) did not take part in the eucharist 'because they do not admit that the eucharist is the flesh of our Saviour Jesus Christ, which suffered for our sins, which in his goodness the Father raised up' (*Letter to the Smyrnaeans*, 7). Even if, as some scholars have argued, this letter was written later in the second century, and not in the 110s as is usually thought, it testifies to an important sharpening of eucharistic language compared with the New Testament, especially given that Ignatius is much more explicit than the New Testament about asserting that Jesus was God; he is therefore implicitly identifying the eucharistic elements as the flesh and blood of God incarnate. Irenaeus makes a similar point, asserting that when the eucharist is received, human flesh and blood are nourished by the flesh and blood of the Lord and prepared for immortality, thus making nonsense of the gnostic view that the flesh will not be saved (*Against Heresies*, bk.4, ch.18; bk.5, ch.2).

The second idea characteristic of later thinking about the eucharist which begins to emerge in the second century is of the eucharist as a sacrifice. At first, this probably did not carry with it the implication that the bread and wine themselves become a sacrifice when they are offered to

God with prayer; rather, the idea of sacrifice was applied to the whole of the eucharist as a way of describing the devotion of those who took part. Often this idea is supported by the quotation of Malachi 1:11: 'For from the rising of the sun to its setting my name is great among the nations, and in every place incense is offered to my name, and a pure offering' (NRSV), which is used, among second-century authors, by the *Didache* (ch.14), Justin (*Dialogue with Trypho the Jew,* 41), and Irenaeus (*Against Heresies,* bk.4, ch.17). In both Justin and Irenaeus, the idea of 'pure offering' is used to contrast the spiritual worship of Christians (identified with the gentiles or 'nations' of the text from Malachi) with the animal sacrifices formerly (before the destruction of the Jerusalem Temple) offered by Jews, which Christians believed God no longer required. (Generally speaking, early Christians sought to argue that their practices and beliefs were parallel to but better than those of the Old Testament and Judaism, or that Judaism in general had been superseded by the new covenant with humanity which God had made by means of Jesus. This view of Judaism is often, and rightly, repudiated by modern Christian theologians.)

But once the use of sacrificial language to refer to the eucharist had become established, it was easy for it to become associated more narrowly with the offering of the bread and wine. We see this in the eucharistic prayer of the *Apostolic Tradition*, where the offering of bread and wine is related to the worthiness of the people to serve God, so it is perhaps still not so far from the idea of pure or spiritual offering just referred to. In the course of time, however, the eucharist could come to be seen, in effect if not explicitly, as an act of propitiation or appeasement of God made through the offering of Jesus' body and blood. Another development which helped this idea to gain hold was the tendency of some writers to interpret Christian ordained ministry through the lens of the Old Testament, so that bishops came gradually to be seen as equivalent to the High Priests of Israel, and the sacrifices of the Old Testament as 'types' or foreshadowings of the eucharist. Tertullian refers to the eucharist as a sacrifice and to bishops as priests (*sacerdos* in Latin) quite frequently, but it is Cyprian of Carthage, in the middle of the third century, who takes the development of thought a stage further, using the language of sacrifice to show that the bishop's action in offering the eucharist imitates what Christ (as high priest – a piece of Old Testament typology) achieved by giving his own life on the cross for the salvation of human beings:

For if Jesus Christ, our Lord and God, is himself the chief priest of
God the Father, and has first offered himself a sacrifice to the Father,
and has commanded this to be done in commemoration of himself,
certainly that priest truly discharges the office of Christ, who
imitates that which Christ did; and he then offers a true and full
sacrifice in the church to God the Father, when he proceeds to offer
it according to what he sees Christ himself to have offered.
Letter 62/63.14

Cyprian perhaps meant only to underline the importance of following
the exact command of Jesus as set out at the Last Supper (something
which, as we have seen, was not so important in the *Didache* over a
century before); but language such as that used in this passage opened the
way to much stronger doctrines of eucharistic sacrifice, as re-presenting
or invoking the sacrifice of Christ on the worshippers' behalf. The
development of a doctrine of eucharistic sacrifice of this sort in medieval
Catholicism was one of the things which made the doctrine of the
eucharist such a bone of contention during the Protestant Reformation,
because it was seen by Protestants as denying that Jesus' death on the
cross was, by itself, enough to secure salvation but required the
eucharistic sacrifice to complete it or to perpetuate its effects.

When considering the relationship of these early doctrines to later
theology, it is important to strike a balance: to acknowledge the early
origin of ideas such as the eucharist as sacrifice, but not to exaggerate the
degree of precise theological thinking already attained by early writers.
For example, the identification of the bread and wine with the body and
blood of Christ does not imply that early writers entertained any theory
as to how this occurred along the lines of the Catholic doctrine of tran-
substantiation (a word which should never be used with reference to the
eucharistic theology of the early church) or of Reformation doctrines
of the 'real presence' of Christ in the eucharist. Among second-century
authors, Justin comes closest to offering an explanation (though what he
says could be supported from others, notably Irenaeus). In the account of
Christian worship which he gives in his *First Apology*, Justin writes of the
eucharistic bread and wine that:

We do not receive these things as common bread or common drink;
but, just as our Saviour Jesus Christ, being incarnate through the
word of God, took flesh and blood for our salvation, so too we have

been taught that the food over which thanks have been given by *a word of prayer which is from him*, from which our flesh and blood are fed by transformation, is both the flesh and blood of that incarnate Jesus.
First Apology, 66

Thus he saw a parallel between the incarnation, by which God's Son became incarnate as flesh and blood through God's word (i.e. his promise or command), and what happens when bread and wine are made into the body and blood of Jesus by *a word of prayer which is from him*. But the italicized phrase is vague and leaves Justin's exact meaning (as perhaps he intended) uncertain. Some scholars have argued that he meant to refer to the use of Jesus' words of institution as a prayer of consecration, effecting a change in the elements, as in the theology of the Catholic and some other churches down to the present day. This, however, is unlikely, since this particular understanding of consecration or change in the elements is not otherwise found until late in the fourth century. The quotation of the words of institution in the eucharistic prayer of the *Apostolic Tradition* does not seem to imply any prayer for consecration or change but only a commemoration of the event of the Last Supper, and no other second or third-century author seems to allude to the use of the institution narrative in a way which would support a stronger interpretation. It is likely, there-fore, that Justin's 'word of prayer' is merely a vague or general reference to the contents of the eucharistic prayer, and does not specify particular words by which a change in the bread and wine was effected.

Many of the features of early Christian worship which we have noted so far are confirmed by sources from later in the third or early in the fourth centuries – including those to which we have unfortunately been able to pay little attention, such as the kiss of peace (noted above in the baptismal eucharist), preaching, and the common meal, now fully distinct from the eucharist, which is discussed at some length in the *Apostolic Tradition*. But there is little further evidence from the pre-Constantinian period for new developments in the way in which the eucharist was celebrated, or for any radical new departures in the theology of the eucharist compared with what we have already described. Strongly realist doctrines of the eucharist continue to co-exist with more 'spiritual' doctrines, which placed less emphasis on the bread and wine as transforming and more on the spiritual worthiness of the recipient. (An example of a theologian who was less realist in his thinking is the

Egyptian Origen [c.185–254], often considered the most important theologian of the pre-Constantinian church.)

The situation changes dramatically in the fourth century, when we have much more evidence for the forms of worship and the doctrines associated with it, and worship itself changed rapidly in response to the new situation of the Roman empire under Constantine and his Christian successors. As we have already noted it is not possible to consider the evidence in detail, but some assessment of the changes may be offered.

Whereas for most of the previous centuries Christian communities had been small, they now grew rapidly in numbers and also often in wealth, and the pressure of numbers in itself led to changes in the pattern of Christian worship. From some point in the fourth century it ceased to be the case that the majority of Christians were baptized and regular recipients of the eucharist; the evidence suggests that many went through most of their lives without seeking baptism, as more-or-less permanent catechumens (a term for the unbaptized who were undergoing instruction). Fourth-century preachers encouraged their congregations to seek baptism, but it is doubtful how successful they were, especially since for anyone who committed a serious sin after baptism the consequences were still serious, at least until penitential discipline was relaxed, beginning at the end of the fourth century: a long period of arduous fasting and humiliation was required before the offender's previous status as a participant in the eucharist was restored. Baptism was a risk which many people were unwilling to take.

To this disincentive to baptism should be added the inaccessibility of churches to many would-be Christians, since the provision of worship-space in the cities of the empire almost certainly failed to keep pace with the growing Christian population during the fourth century. This situation of lack of contact with the sacraments of baptism and the eucharist for the majority of Christians endured for at least half a century, and only began to change as infant baptism became the norm, and so the category of unbaptized Christian gradually disappeared – at least where Christianity was the religion of the vast majority of the population and there were few adult converts left to become catechumens. When this happened is, like so much else, a matter of debate, but Christianity probably did not become the religion of the majority of the population of the Roman empire until around 400, and, as a related development, infant baptism may have begun to become more common around the same date.

Against this slightly negative picture must be set the seriousness with which the fourth-century church seems to have taken the instruction of those who did decide to seek baptism. The century's preoccupation with correct doctrine (in an era when doctrinal struggles took up much of the bishops' time and often required the emperor's attention) is reflected in the careful explanations of the creed, the Bible, and the sacraments of baptism and the eucharist which are found in lectures preached either to candidates for baptism or the newly baptized. For the first time, we have evidence that candidates were required to learn the creed before baptism. Baptism itself became a much more complex ritual, lasting a whole night (plus ceremonies of exorcism and other preliminaries over the previous days) and invested with an aspect of mystery as its recipients were initiated into what had become an exclusive inner circle of faith accessible only to the most committed and pious. There is no doubt that at this period baptism came to share some of the characteristics of the pagan mystery cults, and the word 'mystery' itself came to be, in Greek-speaking Christianity, a term for the sacraments. The rituals and wording of baptism and the eucharist were kept secret from the uninitiated, and the performance of the rites, by an increasingly numerous and profes-sional clergy, in a context, as the church's wealth grew, of increasing architectural and artistic splendour, was invested with as much of a sense of mystery and awe as possible – which visitors to surviving ancient baptisteries in cities such as Ravenna can well appreciate.

If full participation in the eucharist was limited to a small number of baptized Christians, other forms of worship were required to satisfy the spiritual needs of those who, responding to the steady pressure of propaganda, prestige, and sometimes coercion, had attached themselves to the church but remained unbaptized. Here too the influence of pagan religions was important. Christianity adopted many practices formerly connected with pagan religious shrines into the cult or worship of the saints, particularly the martyrs of the first three centuries but increasingly also monks, bishops, and other famous Christians of the Constantinian era itself. The cult of the saints was more ancient than the fourth century (its roots can be traced to the second, when the anniversaries of the deaths of the martyrs were already celebrated), but such phenomena as graveside celebrations, the practice of incubation (seeking healing by sleeping in or near the shrines of saints), and the use of incense and votive candles and other objects (gifts offered to the shrine) began to develop much more rapidly during the Constantinian era. It can also be argued, with some plausibility, that the increasing reverence paid to the Virgin Mary (not particularly evident in the fourth century, but clearer from the fifth onwards) reflected Christian imitation of the reverence paid to goddess figures in various pagan cults.

These developments did not of course serve the needs only of the unbaptized: baptized Christians, including bishops and powerful and wealthy laity, were enthusiastic participants in and patrons of the cults of the saints. Perhaps some of these lay people were finding that formal worship, with greater ceremony, less audibility, and a greater (spiritual as well as physical) distance between clergy and laity, required the supplement of a more personal relationship with the supernatural such as the cult of the saints was able to provide. We are certainly, by the end of the fourth century, a long way from what appears to be the simplicity and fellowship of early Christian worship.

Nonetheless it would be too simple to argue, as is sometimes done, that the practices that have been mentioned in connection with the cult of the saints indicate the continued covert worship of pagan gods – a pagan underground within Christianity. Perhaps sometimes they do, but it is equally possible to see them as vehicles of sincere Christian devotion using aids to worship which responded to genuine spiritual needs and could quite easily be transferred from one religious tradition to another. Bishops and theologians (in sermons which were, at least sometimes, heard by ordinary laity) remained implacably opposed to the polytheism and lack of religious authority of pagan cults, in opposition to which the monotheism and doctrinal uniformity of Christianity, supervised by the clergy, was held up as a virtue.

To conclude then: over the early centuries, Christian worship did undergo a process of formalization, and some features of pagan religious practice became accepted within Christianity. In relation to the eucharist in particular, from the second and early third centuries developments were taking place in practice and theology, that is, the 'realist' identification of the bread and wine with Jesus' body and blood and the doctrine of eucharistic sacrifice, which led eventually to the eucharistic thought characteristic of medieval, especially Western Catholic Christianity. These developments were not by any means unnatural or alien to Christian theology – it was not difficult for them to emerge and be accepted; but, early though their origins were, combined with the growing size and wealth of the church from the fourth century, which distanced clergy from laity and led to a more formal and ritualized form of worship, they changed the nature of Christian worship compared with the New Testament. The scene was set for the further changes of the early Middle Ages, when (in the West) the language of worship ceased to be the vernacular and the reception of communion became a rarity for most Christians. These developments, however, long post-date the era of the early church.

Further Reading

The *Didache*, letters of Ignatius, and some other relevant early Christian texts will be found in M. Staniforth and A. Louth, *Early Christian Writings* (Penguin; second edition, 1987) as well as in *A New Eusebius* (see further reading to Chapter 3). For a collection of early Christian texts specifically relating to the eucharist see R. C. D. Jasper and G. J. Cuming, *Prayers of the Eucharist: Early and Reformed* (Pueblo; third edition, 1987) (the translation of the eucharistic prayer of the *Apostolic Tradition* in this chapter is taken from this book).

There are numerous general studies of early Christian worship, including Paul Bradshaw, *Early Christian Worship: A Basic Introduction to Ideas and Practice* (SPCK, 1996) and Gordon S. Wakefield, *An Outline of Christian Worship* (T. & T. Clark, 1998). An account of early Christian worship complementary to the one in this chapter (though inevitably with some overlaps) will be found in Richard A. Burridge and Graham Gould, *Jesus Now and Then* (SPCK, 2004), ch.7. Many insights into Christian borrowings from pagan religion from the fourth century onwards are supplied by Ramsay MacMullen, *Christianity and Paganism in the Fourth to Eighth Centuries* (Yale University Press, 1997).

Chapter 8
Who Were the Heretics and What Did They Believe?

Lionel Wickham

Some Definitions

The word 'heresy' often means an opinion, usually a valid opinion, which goes against the consensus. That is not what it meant originally. The Greek word from which 'heresy' derives meant, primarily, a 'sect' or 'party' distinguished by a particular programme of ideas. It is used in the New Testament of the Sadducees and Pharisees, and outside the Bible too of 'schools' of thought: as one might talk of 'Marxist' or 'Keynesian' 'schools' of economists and economic theory. The word, in this sense, passes no value judgement on persons or principles. But there is a secondary meaning which the word came to bear and which is also found in the New Testament: 'partisanship' or 'partisan', meaning advocacy of discreditable opinions. The word keeps company with 'schism' which means a split or division in the Church. The two notions of 'heresy' and 'schism' are distinct, but since those who share convictions often split from the rest with whom they do not share them 'heretics' are usually 'schismatics' though 'schismatics' are not always 'heretics'. 'Heretics' to their opponents, of course: because you and your friends are never heretics or schismatics; it is, in a Church context, always other people who are! 'The Church of the Fathers'? By that let us mean the period from the beginning of the second century to the eighth in Latin- and Greek-speaking Christianity, but I shall not go beyond the reign of the Emperor Justinian (died 564). I shall be selective because my title invites me to write the whole history of Christianity in this period and I must keep to essentials.

Christianity is a talkative religion and it has often been complained that religion in general is quarrelsome and that mankind would be better off without it. I do not share that sentiment but it is obvious that religions which say that there is a right and a wrong about what to think and how to behave are likely to talk a great deal and evoke disagreements. Such religions, religions with a 'message' or 'revelation', change the world. If there is no right or wrong, there is no true or false either and discussion is pointless because there is no way of making a difference. The word 'orthodoxy', which basically means 'correct' or 'right' opinion is not to be found in the New Testament. That is largely because Christ and his followers in the next couple of generations were strangers to the idea. The New Testament is rich to extravagance in themes, in subtle metaphors and conceits to paint the picture of life under God 'in Christ'. The themes and metaphors often do not fit together in obvious harmony. Even though the writers recall and reprehend perceived false notions calling them 'superstitious myths' and the like, correct opinion about how the themes and metaphors are to be combined and how they are to be related to the rest of human experience, or to use a wider term, 'correct belief', lies outside their field of vision. To put it in another way: there is no formal theology or Church doctrine in the Bible.

So when did 'opinion' or 'belief' begin so that it could be correct and that there could be Christian 'schools of thought' advocating 'false' opinions? The word 'orthodoxy' in a general sense is not in evidence till the third century. Moreover, 'orthodoxy' is somewhat of an abstraction and, you might say, ever in process of creation, for 'correct belief' has a habit of changing subtly so that what is the Christian consensus comes often to be so no longer. That change is usually called 'development', which is a helpful word to use provided it does not mask the fact that change has taken place or suggest that some idea or practice has just 'rolled out' (the basic meaning of the word) like a carpet, say. Indeed one way of characterizing 'heresy' in a similar general sense is as 'stranded orthodoxy'. Nobody will see a female bishop of Rome in the near future but when and if it happens there will surely be a group of 'heretics' protesting that Church office is not open to women because it never has been. That 'because' betrays the 'heretic' left behind complaining about change while the ship of Orthodoxy sails on. Not all 'heresies' have been like that, but some certainly were cherished explanations and modes of thought overtaken by changes of attitude. The notion of 'orthodoxy', I think we must say, is formed dialectically by relation to 'heresy'. Perhaps you might even call it a privative concept: the absence of heresy or perceived false opinion and belief. So, to repeat the question, when did 'opinions', let us call them 'doctrinal opinions', that could be perceived as false, start? I give the best answer I can but it is contentious for the question is vexed: I judge we should date the start to the early second century. The generation of the Apostles had died (romantic tales were to be written about them not long after) and their legacy, passed on to successors now dead, was fixed in writing. At that point it became possible to speak and argue about ideas and to promote doctrinal opinions about God, the world and their relation in Jesus Christ. In a word, Christian theology came into being: not Christian literature, of course, for the New Testament writings and those of the so-called Apostolic Fathers take precedence, but theology which relates Christ in thought globally (and more than globally – cosmically!) to the whole of existence.

The beginnings of Heresy and Orthodoxy: Gnostics and Gnosticism

Later generations of Catholic theologians (I use 'Catholic' to designate what became the consensus) were to look back on their first forebears as heretics of the worst sort: unkindly and unhistorically, for without the pioneering labours of these 'heretics' they themselves could have done nothing. The received modern name for them is 'Gnostics' and for what are thought to be the characteristics of their style and method, 'Gnosticism'. The name deceives if it suggests uniformity or something as precise as a Church or Religion. Nor has a definition been given which distinguishes Gnosticism uniquely. It is a bit like trying to distinguish between superstition and religion. Every definition I have ever seen makes Catholic Christianity a particular case of Gnosticism. Of course you may argue that it is so: religion is just another name for superstition and Catholic Christianity simply a version of Gnosticism. In that case, you will have to suppose that there is or was something widespread for it to be a particular case of. But what? The answers get vague and arbitrary: 'tendency', 'movement' and the like. However, the name is not pointless and there are themes or traits which it rightly indicates. One important trait is this: the idea that 'Gnosis', or 'knowledge' of divine mystery is to be sought above all things and Christian gnostics hold that it is Jesus Christ's special gift to mankind in the Church. (You will see that this is not a defining feature of 'Gnosticism' over against 'Catholic Christianity' because the New Testament writers frequently speak about 'knowledge of God'.) When I look briefly later at *The Gospel of Mary* which has been thought 'gnostic' and is of interest as figuring in *The Da Vinci Code*, some of the difficulties about the detection of 'Gnosticism' will become apparent. For though there is plenty of evidence of religious groups each with a common myth and spiritual ideals and with affiliations to various teachers (the heresologists have much to say about them and we have a budget of texts stemming from such groups), of immediate interest here are only those which claim connection with Jesus Christ and the literary legacy of the Apostles. Here I am going to leave out of account much that would be of importance if we are looking at the whole picture of religious life in the early Christian centuries. I shall say nothing of the documents found at Nag Hammadi. They are largely irrelevant to our present purpose, fascinating and exasperating though they are in many ways. I will simply state my judgement that in discussing 'Gnosticism' we should take, as the point of reference, what we know of the ideas of theologians who undoubtedly counted themselves as belonging to the tradition stemming from Christ's apostles. Such were Valentinus (an Alexandrian who lived and taught in Rome from the 130s to the 150s), Basilides (who taught at Alexandria at about the same period) and Marcion of roughly the same period too. Marcion was, so we are told, excommunicated from the Church of Rome about 144 and subsequently founded a Church which lasted until the time of the Emperor Justinian in the sixth century; he is different from the other two for that reason, but shares similar features. (See also Chapter 5.)

Reading through the accounts of the doctrinal opinions of these men is rather like seeing a well-known play in a new and idiosyncratic production: the words are readily recognizable but the style and the décor are strange and the interpretation of the plot bizarre; and that is a mark of the success of the consensus which came to prevail. All three taught that what Christ brings is rapport and reconciliation with ultimate reality; however, the creation of the world order, including human beings, and its transformation in Christ depend, they said, on different principles. The god of creation and the Father of our Lord and Saviour Jesus Christ are, they taught, different and contrasted beings. To take Marcion first. He underlined the negative features of the Old Testament to which St. Paul had given attention: the old covenant was mediated through angels and had now been superseded. For Marcion it was the work of a malevolent power, ignorant and vindictive. The Father of Jesus was pure love and generosity bearing no relation to all that so-called 'law' and 'justice' with which Jews and Judaizers concerned themselves. Marcion was not interested in the philosophy of it all. One of his followers said, in reply to questioners, that the important thing was to stick to the Crucified and nothing in the end mattered. The questioners found that comic! St. Paul was Marcion's hero, the expositor of the true and pure gospel which Luke,

St. Paul's companion, had preserved, though it had to be purged of the Jewish bits other people had added. (This estimate of St. Paul will come perhaps as a surprise to people who think of St. Paul as harsh and judge-mental in comparison with Christ. But read the gospels with care and you will notice that though Christ's life of ministry is shown as compassionate and caring, his words are biting and almost inexpressibly demanding: those who did not follow his way would, he is reported to have said, cer-tainly go to Hell and be punished for ever. It was the person and ministry of Christ as the Heavenly Father's means of general reconciliation that St. Paul interpreted rather than Christ's words, which perhaps, indeed, he may not have known all that well. (After all, the gospels were not written until after Paul's death.) Valentinus and Basilides, on the other hand were moved by concepts of Ultimate Reality, by the inexpressible mystery of divine being and the intuitive awareness of the self in relation to the divine. For both, Ultimate Reality is an unknowable nothingness which transcends thought and experience and impinges only indirectly upon this perceptible world order. That order was the product of accident and assuredly not the product of any will of Ultimate Reality to create it. Anthropomorphic notions of personal will have no place, for them, in Ultimate Reality. Parables, allegorical myths and a reading between the lines of the Bible story disclose the mystery of creation and the purpose of Christ's coming. The creation, as we now experience it, is understood as the work of inferior mediating powers. Its material, bodily aspects, and those features and subjects that are untouched by consciousness and a good will, are destined for destruction. For the cosmic, indeed super-cosmic, story is of return to the condition that obtained before the accident of creation. What Christ's coming does is to awaken in spiritual selves ('gnostics') their intuitive awareness of destiny and true being and to offer help to selves of lower grade. For Valentinus these latter are ordinary, common-or-garden church people who need crude things like sacraments; they will never experience that intuition or the bliss it brings but will have some place in the final scheme of things. For Basilides, the end of it all will be the sublime uncon-sciousness of spiritual inequality, a profound and satisfying ignorance.

I have set down a simplified outline of thoughts and themes but enough to show that what these thinkers are concerned with is the programme of questions for all subsequent theology, at least in its basic aspects. Who and what is God? Can God be known? Why is there a world of incarnate spirits? Why is there anything besides spirits? What started it all? How is the whole process going to end? What has Christ to do with the beginning and the end? What is the purpose of the Church? Some things at least are obvious: these questions are puzzling and fascinating and permit of answers after a fashion; this 'gnostic' view of things is schizoid, with insurmountable divisions between body and spirit, God and the World, knowledge and ignorance. Moreover, it might suit study-groups of spiritual snobs sitting at the feet of intellectually adventurous gurus, but not those who had to face the suspicious non-Christian world as a Church. 'Orthodoxy' and 'Church' are connected notions and became actual together: as the churches consolidated, so did their versions of Christian profession. The orthodoxy emerging in the second century rested on elements common to the thinkers I have named and to their critics. To tell the history of that emergence adequately lies outside my remit. It must suffice to say that it came about through the work of thinkers who presented public justifications for Christianity ('Apologists') of whom Justin Martyr (c.100–163/7) is the most important, and through the bishop of Lyons, Irenaeus (c.140–202). Almost all that was to consti- tute 'orthodoxy' for the Church of the Fathers finds its place, at least in germ, in these two writers. They reasoned that God the Creator is the Father of the Lord Jesus Christ, his Son and Word revealed in the Old Testament and actualized in a human body; and that both body and spirit are involved in the cosmic and super-cosmic 'restoration' of all things in Christ. Affirmation of ideas promoted to the agenda, so to say, by 'Gnosticism' accompanied modification or repudiation. Modified was the body–spirit antithesis, for example; repudiated was the use of mythical extensions of the New Testament in 'apocryphal' gospels and the like and affirmed the notion of Christ's work as restoration of an ideal condition lost through error and failure. Many issues were left open and unresolved in the 'patristic' period as a whole, never mind during this earliest phase. But 'heresy' had been disclosed and 'orthodoxy' created. A third out- standing writer I must mention here: Origen (c.185–254) who had been a pillar of orthodoxy in his lifetime but three centuries after his death became a condemned heretic. I leave him till later.

The Gospel of Mary – A Brief Characterization

This is a short Coptic text from the so-called *Gnostic Codex* dated to about 300, in the Berlin Staatsbibliothek. It had been around for more than 50 years before it was first published in 1955. A few bits probably from the third century are also extant in the original Greek and what we have now is about half the piece: of the original 19 pages the first 6 are missing, as are pages 11–14. The colophon ('tail piece') names the text 'The Gospel according to Mary'. As Esther A. De Boer, the most recent editor, argues, 'Mary' is Mary Magdalene. Dan Brown gave it some notoriety in *The Da Vinci Code*. His story supposes that a gnostic gospel has preserved the truth that Mary Magdalene was Jesus' wife, who bore him a child and was his Church's future chosen head. No such cheerful fancy is to be found in the *Gnostic Codex*. Our piece is not a 'gospel' in the sense of a narrative of Jesus' earthly life, works and teaching, but a short fragment of an address by the risen Saviour to the disciples about matter, sin and passion. After it the Saviour departs and the group falls to discussing his words at the invitation of Mary, acknowledged as his most beloved disciple and the privileged recipient of his teaching. Peter doubts her testimony but the other disciples back her up, and thus fortified they go out to preach.

Is this piece 'gnostic'? It is certainly about the Saviour's imparting of knowledge in the form of teaching which demands discussion, interpretation and acceptance. It has a post-Resurrection setting unknown to the New Testament which makes it like other 'apocryphal' gospels and acts which were only in favour for a comparatively short time as 'devotional' reading and not for Church worship. I do not see anything peculiar to the schools of Valentinus or Basilides or anybody else. I regret the absence of so much of the text, but the piece is a trifle bland and soporific despite its brevity. I do not think anybody ever took it as historically true. You have to imagine a great deal to turn it into a gnostic manifesto on feminine spiritual leadership or view its loss as the casualty of Roman Catholic censorship jealous of its privileged access to Truth.

Conflict, Controversy and Prosecution in the Church of the Empire

I leave these early years of Christian history and thought to pass on to the time when Christianity was no longer a protest group with a subversive ideology linked to a programme of social welfare, but had become a large and expanding structured force constituting a loose-knit empire within the Empire. By the beginning of the fourth century there were a lot of

Christians in evidence. Nobody knows how many, just as nobody knows how many inhabitants of the whole Roman Empire there were at the time. It depends what you mean by 'Christians', of course, but let us mean people connected with a worshipping community who expected to receive the support (moral, financial and pastoral) and to undertake some of the responsibilities which that connection entailed. Most sizeable towns had a bishop (and by that I mean a Catholic bishop) with a staff of inferior clergy; the Churches of Rome, Alexandria and Antioch had duties and responsibilities towards the Churches in their provinces to whom they mediated the holiness of the apostolic founders. I say this ecclesiastical empire was 'loose-knit', because even in the time of Justinian (died 564) when the Church was far more strictly regulated than it had been 250 years before, there was room for many local variations of practice and eccentricities. The attempt to suppress Christianity made by the emperor Diocletian had failed and the conversion of Constantine (sole emperor 324–337) and the subsequent adoption of Christianity as the ideology of the Empire, encouraged, and indeed demanded, conformity with fixed standards of belief; for the emperors who undertook the protection of the finances and the good order of the Church in society needed to know who constituted the Church, and that entailed the establishment of defining standards. But the Imperial Church was never a monolithic structure. A series of Ecumenical Church Councils, beginning with Nicaea (325) and including the fundamental Council of Chalcedon (451), propounded such standards in relation to belief about God in Trinity and the person of Christ. But there was always room for dispute and the conciliar definitions never covered everything. Heresies could always arise and the State might be invoked to suppress them.

It was, then, because of the role of the State in relation to the Church that prosecution for heresy and punishment occurred. To speak very generally, Emperor and Church had different functions which might overlap but did not merge. The Church defined 'orthodoxy' as against 'heresy', but the Emperor took the necessary steps to ensure that 'orthodoxy' prevailed; he was expected not to interfere with its contents. The theory was that the Emperor ought to ensure that the contagion of heresy did not spread, not that he should diagnose the ailment. There were limits, too, to the Emperor's powers. Nobody during this period was punished with death solely for his heretical beliefs; but the State might exile dissidents, confiscate property belonging to heretical bodies and ordain penalties for their adherents. These extended in extreme cases to the loss of all civil rights as we might call them. If the heresy had led to a sufficiently large schism the Emperor was left in a quandary. Correspondingly there was no attempt to impose Catholic Christianity by force. Certainly during this period from the early third century to the sixth limits were increasingly imposed on the practice of the old religions and in the days of Justinian in particular on the liberties of the Jews but they fell far short of forcible mass baptisms and the like. Certainly too there were many who took no notice of the new religion and went about their ways as though it had never happened. Nonetheless, what started out with Constantine as positive discrimination in favour of Catholics ended by the time of Justinian in penalties for non-Catholics.

I think that the rule holds good for the Patristic Church as (arguably) for the Church at all times that if in doubt you can always tell which is the Catholic Church: it is the one that persecutes because it invokes the force of the State and prosecutes under the law. Paradoxically, the fact that there might be severe penalties for heresy strengthened Christian intellectual life. Anybody may say what he likes provided he is (shall we say?) 'insincere' and it costs him nothing. The possibility of exile for refusing to conform makes it worthwhile to weigh one's words and the value they then have is both moral and at the same time, as it were, negotiable. The modern heretic, usually a bishop or professor of theology, who weeps all the way from official condemnation to the TV studio and thence to the bank, has his precursor in the Patristic period; and exile, I must add, need not be absolutely intolerable. Heretics then, even persecuted heretics, are not necessarily admirable and selfless rebels for a cause. There are then, I suggest, a number of competing considerations to be borne in mind in relation to the admitted ills of persecution for heresy.

Three Examples: Paul of Samosata, Eunomius and Origen

I want to illustrate the kind of teaching which was officially accounted heresy in this period so that it attracted condemnation by the Catholic Church (which is not necessarily and exclusively the Church of Rome) and fell foul of the law. I propose to deal with people and ideas which had a fair-sized following. The heresologist Epiphanius (365–403) bishop of Salamis, present day Famagusta, used his wits to detect 80 varieties

of heresy most of which probably existed but some of the dottier he
may have made up. They, or at least the chatty bits, make interesting
reading; but the examples I shall look at here will be significant as typical
of the invention of heresy and of its consequences for the formation
of consensus.

My first example comes from the period before the conversion of
Constantine. Paul was from Samosata (in present-day eastern Turkey,
on the Euphrates north-west of Urfa) and became in 260 bishop of the
half a million strong capital city of Coele-Syria, Antioch, a vital centre
of Christianity and the place where, as Acts of the Apostles 11.26
reports, the name, 'Christians', had first been given them. A couple of
centuries later you could call it a Christian city, but not in Paul's time.
His episcopate coincided with the ultimately unsuccessful pretension of
Palmyra to an independent kingdom under Zenobia (261–272), and Paul
is credited with holding office as ducenarius. Whether that is quite true
and what that office involved is not clear: the information we have about
Paul is derived from his opponents: and that is typical of notices about
heresy especially before the fourth century. What we have is a letter to
the bishops of Rome and Alexandria from the Synod, or Church Council,
of bishops constituting the court which tried and deposed him. This gives
Paul's self-aggrandisement together with his arrogant and posturing
behaviour as grounds for the deposition. It mentions, too, that Paul
teaches that Christ is 'from below' (i.e. of human origin) and that he has
espoused the views of someone called Artemas of whom nothing reliable
is known. The bishops say that they might have been prepared to put
up with the undignified behaviour had it not been for Paul's heresy.
You might suspect that the complaint of heresy masks personal jealousies
and rivalries. Of course it could have been so in this case, but those were
times (so different from ours!) when blasphemy or alleged blasphemy
was a serious business. Indeed there is evidence that, more often,
accusations of misconduct masked complaint of supposedly wrong
belief. Whether or not we entertain the suspicion, the way the Council
presents its case to the Christian world beyond Antioch is to clinch
matters with appeal to wrong belief as the ground for deposition. We
may take them at their word: they could have got rid of him on proven
grounds of misconduct, but his unorthodoxy unfitted Paul for office and
(I gloss the words) rendered him a danger to his people. What was his
heresy? From the scraps of information we have of the proceedings it can
reasonably be inferred that Paul explained Christ's Godhead from the

descent of the eternal Word upon him at his baptism by John in the Jordan. Christ is essentially an ordinary ('merely a') man who has been raised to divine status by association; and in this way, too, is the divine Word personalized and individuated. An actual Trinity of Father, Son and Holy Ghost was created by the Father's 'adoption' of Jesus son of Mary. ('Adoption' is my gloss.) This sort of explanation was not entirely new but clearly Paul gave it a fresh turn. He must have been a thoughtful and questioning mind to have worked it through. Later generations were to look back on it as illustrating two cardinal errors: making the being of God subject to process in time; and separating the man, Jesus, from the eternal Word. The condemnation of Paul was upheld by the other great Churches and he was duly deposed. What followed was an unseemly row over the church building which Paul refused to vacate. (This is one of the first references to church buildings; the Church was starting to make claim to public space!) The Emperor Aurelian, now in control after getting the better of Zenobia, was appealed to, and he allocated the church to those in ecclesiastical association with the bishops of Rome and Italy. This did not quite end the matter: a small congregation of Paul's admirers continued for a few years in a city prone henceforth to nourish Christian divisions. Paul's story, his heresy, his deposition and its consequences, illustrate typical features of heresy and orthodoxy some of which I have already remarked. First, heresy and orthodoxy are mostly created by the clergy who had become during the third century the teaching officers of the Church in place of lay gurus. As I have noted above, they could be made to pay the price for getting it wrong; lay people were less open to sanctions. Second, Paul succeeded in calling attention to points of principle which required examination. Moreover the questions he raised could not be settled by simple appeal to traditional authorities: the Bible, or the elements of the Faith learned when someone was prepared for baptism. Once raised they would not go away and answering them was to invent orthodoxy, to develop theology and to change the consciousness first of the Church's intelligentsia and then of simpler believers. Finally, there is the intervention of the (heathen) Emperor ensuring that the Church's decision should hold good and have some real consequences.

My second example is Eunomius and his heresy. He was bishop of Cyzicus (on the Propontis in Western Turkey) in 360 and died c.394. He is the most significant exponent of a doctrine of God which had its roots in the thought of the earliest Catholic theologians. That is a long story, of course. I will just say that by the beginning of the fourth century according to the standard Christian account God the Father, the Eternal Son and Word manifested in Christ Jesus and the Holy Ghost present in believers constitute three distinct subjects. (So Paul of Samosata's explanation was the answer to a reasonable and obvious question.) That century saw what has rightly been called 'a search for the Christian doctrine of God', which is a better name for the ideological aspect of what is otherwise known as the 'Arian' controversy. This controversy was really two searches: for the doctrine of God and for the balanced relation of Church and State. Arius' own words, so far as they are still available, cover a page and a bit; Eunomius left rather more and his theology, though it is similar to Arius' (born about 260 died in 336), owes nothing directly to him. It is a much better worked out version of the same ideas that moved Arius and a good many other thinking Christians of the time. The problem is, how is Jesus Christ 'God'? There was no problem about the Holy Ghost because if you read the Bible strictly (and Eunomius read it extremely strictly as the divine Word expressing itself in the human speech it had created) the Holy Ghost is nowhere in the Bible called 'God'; whereas Christ is. So if Christ is God, then, Eunomius reasoned, he must be so at a secondary level, as a produced, or created God. And if so, the Father, who is his author, is superior to him. Now (and here is the subtle bit) 'Father' does not name the very thing God is, God's substance (God's essential Being and defining characteristics), but the action of God, the divine will. So, though the Son is an utterly faithful likeness of the divine will (i.e., the Father), he is, because he has been produced and created, different from Absolute Godhead. Eunomius did not utter the absurdity that the Son is unlike the Father though that is what you will read in quite respectable text books: nobody in the whole history of Christian thought has ever said that, so far as I know. To gloss Eunomius a little: you can airbrush out the Son and still have a picture of God, who is (more or less in Eunomius' own words) the absolute and divine Being which is and was and will be real whether there be anybody to recognize it or not. Of course it is because of the Son, the creative Word who is the product of ultimate power, that anybody does recognize it and respond. Eunomius believed that the Word had become flesh because Christ's mind was that of the divine Word and Son; such was the general presumption at the time on the part of people who rejected the sort of thing that Paul of Samosata had been saying. You can see why Eunomius rejected any suggestion that the Son was 'the same' or 'like' in 'substance' to the Father: terms that were being mooted in the debates of the time, and the first of which, 'same in substance', had been adopted in 325 at a Council of the Church at Nicaea (Iznik in Western Turkey) convened by Constantine to settle some disputes including that of Arius and his bishop. The Council of Nicaea was just the beginning and the argument among church people went on, becoming more fierce and more political with the Emperor Constantius' (sole Emperor 350–361) attempt to enforce a consensus on stridently quarrelsome bishops and clergy. But there was no consensus; one had to be created and Eunomius was indirectly responsible for its creation. He was ordained bishop in 360, but his diocese did not like him. He resigned and withdrew from communion with his former colleagues, setting up a Church of his own. That was the only way forward for him since his teaching was becoming increasingly old hat. The idea that the eternal Son and Word could best be honoured as 'God' by being explained as a created, secondary God, on a lower level of Being than, and in substance different from, the Absolute God, was coming to seem absurd and frighteningly blasphemous. It frightened the rest of the Church into a consensus formed around the term 'same in substance' (a consensus that has been, with a few exceptions, remarkably stable) and the conviction that Godhead did not admit of degrees or of being created. Besides that, the presumption that Christ had no human mind came under attack because it made him irrelevant to the sinful human mind; and the relevance of Christ to all aspects of human life was (and is) basic to the religion from the time of Irenaeus, who may well have learned it from the Gnostics or at least thought it out under their influence. Eunomius provoked many replies, notably from the group of writers known as the Cappadocian Fathers, Basil bishop of Caesarea, his brother Gregory bishop of Nyssa and Gregory from Nazianzus briefly bishop of Constantinople. They stood Eunomius' theology on its head, so to say, and what they said in reply to him became the orthodoxy that still obtains in the Church generally. State intervention certainly helped to overturn the small Eunomian Church which survived its founder's retirement and death. When Theodosius came to the throne in 378, a new and stricter regime commanded conformity with the faith of Nicaea under penalties for disobedience. In the case of the Eunomians these were extreme, amounting to the loss of the basic Roman (and human) right to inherit property. Gibbon saw that as a cruel joke at the expense of a heresy which separated Father from Son. I think he may have been right, though it was scarcely a joke.

My last example is Origen whom I have mentioned before and I put here because his reputation changed as orthodoxy developed in reaction to his ideas and their consequences. He was a man of extraordinary intellectual vigour, a wonderful teacher about whom legends accumulated even during his lifetime. He ran a sort of Christian academy for entrants to the faith in Alexandria, but left, to the indignation of Demetrius, bishop of Alexandria 189–231, to lecture for a time abroad, and to be ordained priest. On his return to Alexandria he was charged by Demetrius with disobedience and deposed. So he went back to Caesarea in Palestine, where they welcomed him. He died, in some sense a martyr, from the severe treatment he suffered in the persecution in the reign of the emperor Decius (249–251). His legacy to the Church was an enormous body of commentaries on the Bible, sermons, lectures, a defence of Christianity against a hostile critic and a ground-breaking work of philosophical theology *On first Principles*. You could not imagine anybody more orthodox in intention. How was it, then, that three centuries later his reputation was damned? Because he had suggested things no longer politically correct to think. He taught, and indeed had got that idea I have mentioned before into the equivalent of textbooks: that the Son was of a lower Being and status than the Father. He taught too that this created world is a purgatory where everlasting minds are being prepared for their return to the heaven they have abandoned through sinful curiosity bred of boredom with bliss; and he speculated that all would finally be well for all selves in an ever advancing universe. Origen had become improper reading a hundred years after his death but it was to take a further 200 before he was officially condemned. What a shame that condemnation was! Cyril the wise bishop of Alexandria (412–444) and a pillar of tradition disapproved of Origen's ideas but he did not condemn him by name and said that in principle people should not be unchurched after their death within the peace of the Church. The window they gave Origen in the chapel of Emmanuel College, Cambridge scarcely compensates for the ecumenical damnation of his memory.

In sum, then. Heresy was (and is) an inevitable consequence of debate about the meaning of the Christian religion. It created (and creates) that orthodoxy which is the consensus, and which is itself exposed to criticism and change. What was once orthodox could become heresy; the reverse did not, I think, happen and I can think of no examples. Penalties for

heresy under public law came about through the development in the
relation of Church and State. They could be severe but never amounted
in this period to the widespread brutality of medieval and more
recent times.

Further Reading

Extracts in English translation from the literary sources mentioned above can be found
in J. Stevenson and W. H. C. Frend, *A New Eusebius: Documents Illustrating the History
of the Church to* AD *337* (SPCK, 1987) and, by the same authors, *Creeds, Councils
and Controversies: Documents Illustrating the History of the Church* AD *337–461*
(SPCK, 1989). There is additional material to be found in Henry Bettenson, *The Early
Christian Fathers: A Selection from the Writings of the Fathers from St Clement of Rome
to St Athanasius* (OUP, 1956 and reprinted several times) and *The Later Christian Fathers
from St. Cyril of Jerusalem to St. Leo the Great* (Oxford University Press, 1970 and
likewise reprinted). An English translation of *The Gospel of Mary* can be found in *The
Nag Hammadi Library* in English, translated under the editorship of James M. Robinson
(Brill, 1984) and in Esther A. De Boer, *The Gospel of Mary: Listening to the Beloved
Disciple* (Continuum, 2004). For studies of particular themes and authors, consult *The
Oxford Dictionary of the Christian Church*, edited by F. L. Cross and E. A. Livingstone
(Oxford University Press, 1997); *Encyclopedia of the Early Church*, edited by Angelo
di Beradino (James Clarke, 1992); and *The Cambridge History of Christianity: Origins
to Constantine*, edited by Margaret M. Mitchell and Frances M. Young (Cambridge
University Press, 2006).

Chapter 9

What Did Constantine Do for Christianity?

Graham Gould

Constantine, the first Christian Roman emperor, is one of the most controversial figures in the history of the Christian church but also, arguably, one of the most important in the history of Europe. At the beginning of the fourth century, Christianity was the religion of a small minority of the population of the Roman empire (even if it would be wrong to exaggerate its social insignificance); as a result of Constantine's conversion and the changes in the legal and social status of Christianity which followed it, the church was able to grow within a century to a position of religious dominance within the empire, to extend its embrace to the 'barbarian' peoples beyond the empire's European frontiers, and eventually to become the religion which shaped medieval Europe and the birth of the modern world. The history of Western civilization has thus turned to a very large extent on the decision of the emperor Constantine to adopt Christianity as his personal faith and to promote it among his subjects.

In modern times Christians in the West have become accustomed to the idea of living in a 'post-Constantinian' era. The close alliance between church and state which was pioneered in the later Roman empire and was the norm in medieval and early modern Europe no longer holds good. Society and politics have been secularized and the churches have suffered numerical decline and loss of social and cultural prestige. Many churchpeople, far from regretting this, have welcomed it as a liberation from the conditions imposed on the churches by the Constantinian pattern of church – state relations, which can be viewed as having turned the churches into too-keen supporters of the social and political status quo and, over many centuries, impeded their ability to fulfil their vocation to oppose injustice and champion the poor, the oppressed, and the despised. For Christians who take this view, Constantine is one of the villains of church history, who failed to under-stand the true nature of the faith to which he was converted, viewing it as one more tool of political control and neglecting the radical cutting edge of Jesus' teaching.

While there is much to be said against the Constantinian legacy to the church and in favour of a more radical or prophetic interpretation of the relationship between church and society, any assessment of Constantine himself should be based on a proper understanding of the context of his reign and of his reasons for making the church (as it seems to critics) a servant of imperial policy. This brief chapter will discuss Constantine's conversion, his religious policy, and some of its longer term consequences, without, of course, being able to provide the full account of either religious or general history which can be found in specialized books.

Constantine was born, *c.*272, at Naissus on the river Danube (modern Nish in Serbia). His father Constantius, an army officer, was from the Danube province of Dacia, and there is no truth in the idea that Constantine was born in Britain or in the medieval legend that his mother Helena was a British (or Welsh) princess: she was from Drepanum, a town in Bithynia in Asia Minor, and had probably met Constantius when he was stationed nearby. Constantine was, however, in Britain when he was proclaimed emperor by the army at York on 25 July 306, following the death of Constantius, who had risen through the ranks to be appointed Caesar (or co-emperor) in 293. Constantine's path to absolute power was lengthy and involved war against several rivals, but it had two main stages: his defeat of the usurper Maxentius at the battle of the Milvian Bridge, near Rome, on 28 October 312, by which Constantine gained control of the whole of the western Roman empire; and of Licinius at the battle of Chrysopolis, on 18 September 324, which brought him the eastern provinces and left him unchallenged ruler of the empire until his death on 22 May 337.

The empire which fell to Constantine between 306 and 324 had seen a period of long-term instability in the third century, but had been set on a sounder military and economic footing by the reforms of Diocletian (emperor 284–305) and his imperial colleagues. Constantine was to continue the process of recovery, which was to enable the Roman empire, despite the threat of the barbarian invasions, to survive for over a century after his death. Between 303 and 312 persecution directed against Christians had been part of the official policy for enforcing a new unity on the empire, promoted mainly by the eastern emperors Galerius and Maximinus. In the west under Constantius the persecution had been shorter and less violent than in Palestine or Egypt, but nonetheless had produced martyrs and confessors, especially in North Africa. There is evidence that when Constantine became emperor in 306 he repealed the measures which had been taken against the Christians and restored their confiscated property (or at least their freedom to worship) in the part of the empire under his control. At any rate, his personal conversion to Christianity, when it came, was not a reversal of his previous policy towards the church; Constantine was no Paul, converted from persecutor to apostle.

Constantine's conversion, as it is traditionally understood, took place just before the battle of the Milvian Bridge. Two descriptions by contemporaries survive. Lactantius, who a few years later became tutor to Constantine's son Crispus, composed his around 314–315 and Eusebius of Caesarea, the church historian, who met Constantine on a few occasions after 324, included his in his *Life of Constantine*, written after the emperor's death. In a pamphlet attacking the emperors who had persecuted Christianity, Lactantius describes Constantine's final preparations for the decisive battle against Maxentius:

> Constantine was directed in a dream to mark the heavenly sign of God on the shields of his soldiers and then engage in battle. He did as he was ordered and (by means of a slanted [or cross-shaped] letter X, with the top of its head bent round) marked Christ on the shields. Armed with this sign the army took up its weapons.
> *On the Deaths of the Persecutors*, 44.5–6

The phrase in brackets, though not entirely clear, is usually interpreted to suggest that the symbol on the shields was a form of the Chi – Rho monogram (from the first two letters of the name Christ). But it may well have originated as an attempted explanation, and not necessarily an accurate one, added to the text by a copyist, of what would originally have been an allusion to the more simple sign of the cross. Lactantius does not explicitly describe the dream as marking a conversion, but nothing he writes suggests he thought Constantine was a Christian before these events.

Eusebius claims that his account of the conversion came from Constantine himself, who swore to its truth. The emperor wished for divine aid in the battle but was uncertain about which divinity to pray to, before deciding to call on the one God worshipped by his father (not, however, said to have been a Christian):

> And while he was thus praying with fervent entreaty, a most incredible sign appeared to him from heaven... He saw with his own eyes the trophy of a cross of light in the heavens, above the sun,

and an inscription, 'Conquer by this', attached to it… Then [later]
in his sleep the Christ of God appeared to him with the sign which
he had seen in the heavens, and commanded him to make a likeness
of that sign… and to use it as a safeguard in all engagements with
his enemies.
Life of Constantine, 1.28–9

Eusebius and Lactantius have in common the dream and the sign of
the cross, but not the daylight vision of Eusebius' account. It is possible
that the vision, despite the emperor's oath of authenticity, may have
been added to the story in the course of re-telling, with the intention
of emphasizing the public rather than private character of the divine
revelation. But it has also been suggested that the emperor and his soldiers
may have witnessed a solar halo or similar atmospheric distortion.

While many scholars regard the conversion story, in whatever
form is regarded as most original, as historically reliable, a different
interpretation makes it a Christian version of a vision of the god Apollo
which Constantine is described, in a speech written in his honour, as
having experienced two years before. Though the description of the
pagan vision is much less explicit than the Christian one, it is possible
that Christians, wishing to add a supernatural component to the story
of Constantine's decision for Christianity, borrowed or hit upon the
motif of either a dream or vision (or both) to rival the pagan vision –
if the latter was generally known. Another theory is that Constantine's
description of the solar vision in Eusebius' account reflects a family
background in sun-worshipping monotheism. Neither of these theories
should, however, be taken as proof that the story of the conversion is
a fabrication, and that Constantine in fact continued to be a pagan after
312. It is quite clear from his actions not long after the battle of the
Milvian Bridge that he considered himself a Christian from around this
time; though the details of the conversion will always be subject to
historical questioning, Constantine's self-understanding as a Christian
emperor during the rest of his reign was more important in the long run
than how he actually came to the faith.

In 313 Constantine and Licinius (who had recently defeated the last
persecuting emperor in the East, Maximinus) agreed on a policy of
toleration of all forms of worship, but particularly of Christianity.
(The letter stating this policy is often referred to as the 'Edict of Milan'.)
Provincial governors were ordered to restore confiscated property to

Christians – as Constantine had probably already done in the part of the western empire under his control before 312. The motive for toleration given in the edict is to ensure that the emperors receive the favour of 'whatever divinity dwells in heaven' – a general phrase but which to Constantine probably recalled the support he believed he had received from the Christian God at the Milvian Bridge.

Not long after this, we find evidence both of Constantine's support for the churches and of explicit intervention in church affairs. Money was granted to bishops for new buildings and for the support of clergy, who were also granted exemption from public offices, service in some of which was compulsory for wealthy citizens. (Later the provisions of this exemption had to be limited, to prevent rich men seeking ordination to evade civic responsibility.) As in the edict of toleration, but this time in an explicitly Christian context, Constantine makes it clear that the motive for these actions is to allow the clergy to concentrate on their religious tasks of prayer and worship, as a benefit to the state. In a letter to Bishop Caecilian of Carthage about the distribution of funds he shows he is becoming familiar both with the organization of the church and also with an appropriately pious phraseology.

In North Africa the Donatist schism had divided the church into hostile and probably roughly equal parties. The Donatists rejected the ministry of bishops, including Caecilian, whom they believed to have betrayed the faith by compromising with the authorities to avoid imprisonment or martyrdom during the persecution. Probably because it was necessary to decide which group should receive imperial favour, Constantine was drawn into the dispute and first instructed Bishop Miltiades of Rome to conduct an investigation, and then in 314 summoned Caecilian and the leaders of the Donatists to a council of bishops at Arles in Gaul for an adjudication. (The Donatists had requested this location in a letter to Constantine, because, significantly, the Gallic bishops had not been persecuted during Constantius' rule and so had not been tainted by compromise with the state.) But all attempts to resolve the dispute failed, despite attempts to force the Donatists to comply with successive rulings in favour of Caecilian.

The letters connected with the investigation into Donatism show that Constantine was worried that toleration of divisions among Christians would lead to God being less favourable to his rule. A strong belief in providence and his own status as a recipient of divine favour runs through his correspondence for the rest of his reign. Critics can validly make the point that to view Christianity as a cult whose proper performance encourages God to protect the empire falls short of a full appreciation of Christian teaching; there is no doubt, however, that Constantine was by his own lights a sincere believer, even though he was not a baptized member of the church and did not become one until shortly before his death. (As has been explained in the chapter on early Christian worship, many Christians in the fourth century delayed their baptism because of fears of committing a serious sin after baptism and incurring either eternal punishment or at least the rigours of the penitential discipline.)

The danger of church divisions was something which Constantine was to remember when he fell out with Licinius and eventually defeated him to become sole emperor. In Alexandria a dispute had broken out between Bishop Alexander and one of his presbyters, Arius, over the doctrine of the Trinity. But Arius had succeeded in obtaining support from other bishops against Alexander, and a local argument threatened to become a much wider and more disruptive one. This (in very summary form) was the background to the summoning of the Council of Nicaea in June 325, which Constantine intended to serve as a forum for the solution not only of the Arian controversy but of a number of other disagreements which were unsettling the churches. Constantine ordered the Council moved from Ancyra in central Asia Minor to Nicaea in Bithynia so that he could be present: the imperial residence at Nicomedia was close by.

The Council of Nicaea was the first occasion in the history of the church when a large assembly of bishops (over 200 were present) adjudicated on a doctrinal question of really major significance; the first time that a new creed was written to embody their conclusions (creeds had previously been used only in baptismal ceremonies, and were not usually meant to embody technical theological points); and the first time that the threat of deposition and exile, enforced by the state, was used to obtain agreement with the proceedings. These innovations would hardly have been possible without Constantine's interest in the Council (even the travel arrangements of so many bishops needed imperial support) and they set a precedent for further interventions by the empire in doctrinal disputes over the next centuries. The emperor's concern, however, was visible unity, and it is important not to exaggerate the extent to which his personal view of Christianity affected the decisions of the Council. As noted already in the chapter on the Papacy, the decision of the Council of Nicaea to affirm the full divinity of Jesus, the Son of God, was the product of discussions within a Christian theological tradition already centuries old. Constantine is credited by Eusebius of

Caesarea with personally suggesting, or at least supporting, the addition of the word *homoousios* ('of one substance') to the Nicene creed's description of the Son's relationship to the Father. But, even if this is true (and Eusebius may simply be guilty of awe-struck flattery), Constantine was probably acting on the advice of a group of bishops, and the use of the word *homoousios* in the doctrine of the Trinity was not itself new, any more than the belief in Jesus' divinity which it represented. The suggestion that is still occasionally made, that under the influence of Constantine Nicaea reflected the triumph of an essentially 'pagan' view of Christianity as the worship of a pantheon of demi-gods or divine heroes, is as wide of the mark as the view (see Chapter 3) that the Council was under papal control.

From 324 onwards, Constantine's legislation places an increasing emphasis on Christianity as the religion of the empire to which the emperor had a divinely appointed mission to convert his subjects. The toleration which had become official policy in 313 was maintained in that pagans were allowed to retain their temples and none were martyred, but pagan worship as part of official ceremonies or public celebrations was banned and it seems from the evidence of Eusebius' *Life of Constantine* (2.45; 4.23–5) that pagan sacrifices were completely prohibited – though some scholars have doubted that such a drastic step was possible as early as Constantine's reign rather than later in the fourth century. Among many other laws making reference to or promoting Christian values, the observance of Sunday was encouraged and property was confiscated from temples to fund the building of churches. By the end of Constantine's reign, in Rome, Jerusalem, Tyre, and other large cities' new cathedral churches, paid for by the state, advertised the emperor's faith. (Churches in Palestine benefited from Helena's patronage when she made a tour there in 326; but the theory that during her visit she discovered the remains of the cross of Jesus does not appear until the end of the fourth century.)

Of course, the campaign against paganism left many traditional religious practices untouched, and rich pagans were to continue to resist conversion and even to hold office at court for as much as two centuries in the eastern empire (which from the 330s onwards centred on Constantine's new capital city of Constantinople). But (with the exception of the short reign of the pagan emperor Julian, 361–363) with Constantine the official religious policy of the empire had changed for good. In the eastern empire at least, the change in the relative legal position of paganism and Christianity after 324 was swift enough for the label Constantinian revolution or reformation to be considered valid, and the emperor might well be satisfied with what he had achieved – satisfied enough to venture the conceit of telling an assembly of bishops that he too was a bishop, appointed by God over those outside the church (*Life of Constantine*, 4.24).

As has already been remarked in the chapter on worship, the conversion of Constantine, imperial patronage and support, and the increasing Christianization of the empire brought pastoral problems as well as opportunities for the church and led to long-lasting changes in the character of Christian worship, as well as in methods of church government. Three of Constantine's sons, especially the longest surviving, Constantius II (337–361), continued his policy of active intervention in doctrinal disputes and church councils. This led, in the 350s, to opposition to Constantius from those supporters of the Council of Nicaea who resisted his attempts to achieve a compromise between supporters and opponents of the Council by promoting a compromise creed. But towards the end of the century, in the years 379–381, it was the religious policy of the emperor Theodosius I which finally brought about the (almost) universal acceptance of the decisions of the Council of Nicaea by the church, as well as promoting the authority of the Bishop of Rome, who was one of the bishops with whom agreement was decreed to be a test of orthodoxy.

It was also during the reign of Theodosius that a sustained campaign against surviving pagan temples took place, leading often to violence by Christian mobs, and legislation was enacted making both paganism and heresy subject to severe penalties and loss of civil rights. The legislation against heresy continued to be enforced and enhanced during the further doctrinal controversies of the following century. By 395 – the year of Theodosius' death and also of the final division of the eastern and western empires into two separately governed halves – the Roman state was not only officially Christian but had adopted an official orthodoxy based on the creed of Nicaea, and embarked on the persecution of pagans and heretics, often with the enthusiastic support of the church. It was to take centuries of further change to create the close relationship between church and state which, combined with the intellectual dominance of the church and (in the West) the power of the Papacy, gave force to the concept of Christendom: a realm in which religious and political ideology were united in support of the church, dissident views and alternative theologies were suppressed, and Christianity percolated every aspect of social and cultural existence. Nonetheless, the foundations were laid in the reigns of Constantine and his successors; within a century of the battle of the Milvian Bridge the church had moved from the position of persecuted to that of persecutor.

Further Reading

Many historical documents connected with Constantine are to be found in *A New Eusebius* (see further reading to Chapter 3), including the evidence for his conversion, his vision of Apollo, and the Council of Nicaea. Another sourcebook with many interesting fourth-century documents is A. D. Lee, *Pagans and Christians in Late Antiquity* (Routledge, 2000). There is a modern translation of *Eusebius: Life of Constantine* by Averil Cameron and Stuart G. Hall (Oxford University Press, 1999).

There is a very large bibliography on Constantine. Hans A. Pohlsander, *The Emperor Constantine* (Routledge, 1996) is a short study which contains references to older interpretations as well as original sources. Averil Cameron, *The Later Roman Empire* (Fontana, 1993) provides an account of the background to Constantine's reign and the subsequent history of the Christian Roman empire. A more detailed but readable account is T. D. Barnes, *Constantine and Eusebius* (Harvard University Press, 1981). The classic statement of modern Christian hostility to Constantine is Alistair Kee, *Constantine versus Christ: the Triumph of Ideology* (S.C.M. Press, 1982).

Index